WRITING A NOVEL

WRITING A NOVEL

John Braine

Coward, McCann & Geoghegan, Inc.
New York

First American Edition 1974

Copyright © 1974 by John Braine (Bingley) Ltd.

SBN: 698–10584–2

Library of Congress Catalog Card Number: 73–93771

For permission to quote from copyrighted material, the author gratefully acknowledges the following: Houghton Mifflin Co., for excerpts from *Room at the Top* by John Braine, reprinted by permission of Houghton Mifflin Co., publishers; Fawcett Publications, Inc., for an excerpt from *Death of a Citizen* by Donald Hamilton, copyright © 1960 by Donald Hamilton and published by Fawcett Publications, Inc.; Harcourt Brace Jovanovich, Inc., for an excerpt from *The Tyranny of Words* by Stuart Chase, reprinted by permission of Harcourt Brace Jovanovich, Inc., publishers; Alfred A. Knopf, Inc., for excerpts from *Saturday Night and Sunday Morning* by Alan Sillitoe, copyright © 1958 by Alan Sillitoe. Reprinted by permission of Alfred A. Knopf, Inc.; Little, Brown and Company, for excerpts from the omnibus volume, *A Dance to the Music of Time* by Anthony Powell, copyright 1951, 1955 by Anthony Powell, from which excerpts from the novels, *The Acceptance World* and *A Question of Upbringing* have been used, and for excerpts from *A Dance to the Music of Time: Second Movement* by Anthony Powell, including passages from *A Buyer's Market* and *At Lady Molly's*, reprinted by permission of Little, Brown and Company, publishers; New Directions Publishing Corporation for an excerpt from *The Crack-Up* by F. Scott Fitzgerald. Copyright 1936 by Esquire, Inc., copyright © 1964 by Frances Scott Fitzgerald Lanahan. Reprinted by permission of New Directions Publishing Corporation; Random House, Inc., for excerpts from *Ulysses* by James Joyce. Copyright 1914, 1918 by Margaret Caroline Anderson and renewed 1942, 1946 by Nora Joseph Joyce. Reprinted by permission of Random House, Inc.; Random House, Inc., for excerpts from *Appointment in Samarra* by John O'Hara. Copyright 1934 and renewed 1962 by John O'Hara. Reprinted by permission of Random House, Inc., and for excerpts from *From the Terrace* by John O'Hara. Copyright © 1958 by John O'Hara. Reprinted by permission of Random House, Inc.; Charles Scribner's Sons, for excerpts from *The Great Gatsby* by F. Scott Fitzgerald. Copyright 1925 by Charles Scribner's Sons, copyright renewal 1953 by Frances Scott Fitzgerald Lanahan. Reprinted by permission of Charles Scribner's Sons; Simon and Schuster, Inc., for an excerpt from *The Writing of One Novel* by Irving Wallace. Copyright © 1969 by Irving Wallace. Reprinted by permission of Simon and Schuster, Inc., publishers; The Viking Press, Inc., for excerpts from *A Burnt-Out Case* by Graham Greene. Copyright © 1960, 1961, 1966 by Graham Greene. Reprinted by permission of Viking Press, Inc., and for an excerpt from *Phoenix II: Uncollected, Unpublished and Other Prose Works* by D. H. Lawrence, edited by Warren Roberts and Harry T. Moore. Copyright 1925 by Centaur Press, copyright renewed 1953 by Frieda Lawrence. Reprinted by permission of Viking Press, Inc.

Printed in the United States of America

For John Bright-Holmes
with affection and gratitude

FOREWORD

This is a practical manual, a conducted tour of my workshop. The workshop is scruffy—I imagine it as a ramshackle wooden hut on the wrong side of town, every piece of machinery makeshift and battered—but somehow or other the work is done there, and done on time. The rules which I write by are rules of thumb, rough guides rather than precise instructions. I didn't formulate them before I wrote my first novel; I stumbled across them in the process of writing it.

There's a story of the new captain of a ship being shown round his quarters by the retiring captain. He's given a sealed envelope and told to lock it away. Inside that envelope is information which will save him from a terrible disaster. He cannot be forewarned about the disaster, but when it's upon him he'll know what it is and then, and then only, must he open the envelope. The new captain sticks it out for several days, but then curiosity forces him to open the envelope. Inside he finds a slip of paper bearing the words PORT LEFT, STARBOARD RIGHT.

My rules are as simple as that. I'm always opening the envelope and, to carry on the analogy just about as far as it can be carried, always being saved from the disaster of rejection. I don't guarantee that if you follow my rules you'll write a best-seller, much less a masterpiece. (Remember, incidentally, that though all best-sellers are not masterpieces, all masterpieces are best-sellers.) I am sure that, if you have the necessary ability, observing my rules will enable you to write a novel which will be accepted for publication.

John Braine

There isn't, unfortunately, any way of discovering whether you can write a publishable novel except by writing it. You're either born with this particular talent or you're not. You can acquire a decent prose style, a deep knowledge of human nature, and—just as important—of the physical world. You can even acquire facility in devising plots. But if you haven't the ability to sustain a full-length narrative, there's nothing you can do about it.

Intelligence, education, and hard work won't remedy the deficiency. It's terribly unfair, just as life itself is unfair; the sword is plucked from the stone, so to speak, not by the great knight, veteran of a thousand battles, but by the scrawny pageboy. I have known more than one professional writer —well-read enough to make me appear illiterate, intelligent enough to make me appear half-witted—try his hand at a novel. The result has been not without distinction, but dead at the heart, with possible value as autobiography or sociology or philosophy, but none as a novel, none as a story to be read for pleasure.

I may add that it gives me enormous delight when I look at the work of a clever non-novelist and discover it to be a non-novel. The delight is all the keener when the non-novelist is a reviewer.

None of this is irrelevant. You don't know whether you can write a publishable novel until you've written it: You do know whether you've the necessary ability. You are always given the information by your instincts, and your instincts are never wrong. You must not fall into the error that novels can only be written either by the highly educated and highly intelligent or by the fluent and highly competent hacks to whom writing a novel is just a job like any other. There is nothing so crippling as trying to be what by nature you never can be.

What is vital before you've written your first novel, and whilst you're writing it, is to hang on, to endure. Having recognized your vocation is not enough. If you don't think clearly about it, if you don't use your talent in the right way, then it can all come to nothing.

They say genius will out. I've never believed it myself. If a potential heavyweight champion loses an arm, he's not going to be a boxer, and that's that. And if a writer goes in the wrong direction at an early age, he's not going to be a writer. If the hero of *The Queen of a Distant Country* [1] speaks for me nowhere else, he speaks for me here. There is no greater happiness in the world than to be fulfilled in your vocation, even if the material rewards are minimal. There is no greater bitterness than to realize that your vocation has come to nothing, even if you're materially successful. But life awards few consolation prizes: To fail as a writer doesn't automatically mean that you will be successful at anything else.

The novel is the most variable of all literary forms. The minimum length in this country is 40,000 words, and 150,000 the generally accepted maximum. There are no rules about technique or subject matter or purpose. No experimentation is barred, nothing is taboo, the novelist may be as ideologically committed as he chooses. The main reason for this state of affairs is that though the sales of a first novel are generally small, so are the costs of production. The publisher generally breaks even and, the public taste being unpredictable, may make a considerable profit on the most unlikely properties.

A rough, shambling, confused, immature first novel may sometimes be published as it stands, because whilst to revise it might remove its faults, it might also remove its virtues. Or it might be extensively revised—in some cases virtually rewritten—by the publisher. This happens more often in the United States than in England.

I believe that both these extremes can be avoided, that every first novel can be a thoroughly craftsmanlike job, fit to print as it stands. (After the removal, that is, of the numerous small errors which creep into every manuscript.)

John Braine

It isn't merely a matter of acceptance for publication —though I must emphasize that a technically competent job stands the most chance of acceptance. There is the future to be considered. You won't want a novel under your name which you realize you could have made much better. Nor will you want to feel, if the novel has been extensively revised at the publisher's suggestion, that it isn't entirely your own work.

You will, quite naturally, dream of your first novel being a success, as my *Room at the Top* was. You mustn't make any commercial calculations; you mustn't try to find out what the public likes. It's a waste of time. The most that can be said is that the public likes a good story. That's all; the subject or the period is absolutely immaterial. I may also add that no thought at all should be given to whether it will make a film. If it's successful, the film rights will almost certainly be sold. When the film rights of a novel are sold, it isn't a film story which is bought, but an audience. You must write to please yourself; you must be completely honest about the world as you see it.

At the same time, it's absolutely marvellous to write a successful novel. Don't be misled by anyone: Success isn't an empty shell; it's sweet and succulent all the way through. Apart from the money, there is the satisfaction of having your name mean something, of overnight being sought after, of suddenly becoming newsworthy. But in the long run it's only the work that matters; and your period as a literary lion may be short-lived. Strawberries are not nourishing and have little vitamin content; but let us eat as many as we can whilst they're in season.

As far as the choice of subject is concerned, our literary establishment is, of course, absolutely permissive. As far as success is concerned, it is curiously puritanical. It is fiercely prejudiced against the author who is resoundingly successful with his first book. This is held somehow to be not playing fair: Writers should begin by being promising, improve with each succeeding book, and arrive with a mature and deeply felt achievement, not far short of a masterpiece, which penetrates to the heart of the human condition. (What exactly is the human condition I've never been quite sure, but once a reviewer uses the phrase, you're home and dry.)

You must not be influenced by this notion in any way. I don't mean that anyone deliberately chooses not to write a successful first novel or, indeed, that he can be said to have the choice. I mean that he well may diminish his chance of success by thinking of his novel as a trial of his powers, a preliminary canter, by not stretching his talent to its fullest, by putting off the struggle with problems of technique until later novels, by taking the easy way. I can't particularize these problems because they're different for every writer; but every writer will recognize them when he encounters them—they're apparently impossible to solve.

But this far I can particularize: The main deficiency in first novels is sketchiness of treatment. In short, the reader doesn't always hear about what he wants to hear about. It's not a question of mysteries, of the reader purposely not being told. For then he knows that he'll be told eventually. It's a question of his never being told, not being given the full story. The full story, the novel as it should have been written, is there in the author's mind: If it weren't, the reader wouldn't be aware of something missing.

I don't want to dwell unduly on this matter of success, and as I stated in the beginning, I certainly can't promise it to anyone. But let me speak quite plainly. It's nicer to be successful than unsuccessful, and infinitely more satisfactory to be a full-time than a part-time writer. The life of the professional novelist is insecure—though no more so than that of many other professionals—but it confers personal freedom. There are bad moments all along the way, but it is never less than totally absorbing. The financial rewards are generally wildly overestimated, since the majority of people, journalists included, are totally ignorant of the punitive nature of the tax system. Nevertheless, there is always the chance of earning a comfortable living. Certainly anyone who has taken the trouble to learn how to write readably should be able to earn at least 2,000 pounds a year. This isn't much, but it's more than the majority of the working population gets—and gets for jobs which are mostly pretty dreary.

To write a successful first novel doesn't necessarily mean that you'll be able to become a professional writer—nor may you want to. And it isn't all-important that your first novel be successful. But it's very obviously preferable.

Public taste is arbitrary and incalculable, and success may come at any stage of a novelist's life—in fact, if he's unlucky, not until after he's dead. But the chances of success with a first novel are the greatest. Your first novel has a special quality which none of your other novels will have, even if they're far superior. Your voice is a new voice, there has been none like it before. Your story is new because you've never told a story before. You can't tell any story in the same way again, any more than you can lose your virginity twice. Your first novel isn't your only chance of success, but it is your best chance.

Having considered this, put it in the back of your mind. You have now to live with the novel; there can be no room in your mind for dreams of success. It's better to expect nothing, for then you can't be disappointed. You mustn't even think about acceptance or rejection, but only about writing a novel which will satisfy you yourself. This is terribly simple; and I don't use the word "terribly" lightly.

The rules which I lay down for the writing of a novel are the ones which suit me. They certainly aren't going to suit everybody. I don't assert that my way of writing a novel is the best way or the only way; only that it works. Since 1957 I have earned a reasonable living by my novels, and though I have my moments of desperate insecurity, I expect to keep on doing so. My theories are derived from practice, not the other way round. I show you only my own route because it's the only one I know and I'm absolutely sure of its destination. Divergences from it may be possible; other routes may be better for you; but this only your instincts can decide.

Whether my way of writing a novel is acceptable to you or not, there is one warning. It's quite true that there are naturally fluent writers who cannot slow down, who cannot revise. Taking too many pains, thinking too much about the novel, would paralyze them. If you are one of these, remember that those who write quickly learn quickly, and that it's just as easy to do it the right way. Don't ever assume that you have nothing to learn. But I speak here of the minority; for the majority of novelists, the difficult way is the only way. A novelist's vocation is like any other; discipline and technique are infinitely more important than inspiration.

Finally, it's absolutely imperative that you put out of your mind any notion of experiment. The first reason is brutally simple: Experimental novels aren't accepted. The second reason is, strangely enough, even more important: There is nothing which you cannot say within the framework of the straightforward realistic novel. It is the people in your story who should astound us. The great failing of the novel in England is its self-imposed restriction of subject and its stereotyped attitudes toward every aspect of life, particularly class. To be shockingly original with your first novel, you don't have to discover a new technique: Simply write about people as they are and not as the predominantly liberal and humanist literary establishment believes that they ought to be.

xv

ONE: A writer is a person who writes

Once the late Sinclair Lewis arrived at Harvard, drunk as usual (alcoholism is our main occupational disease), to talk about writing. "Hands up, all those who want to be writers!" he yelled. Everyone's hand went up. "Then why the hell aren't you at home writing?" he asked, and staggered off the platform.

I begin with this anecdote because it illustrates a simple but profound truth: A writer is a person who writes. You don't wait to write until you have something to write about. As long as you're of normal intelligence and all your senses are functioning (though even this isn't essential), you have all the material which you need. You don't think before you write. Writing *is* thinking because it's the arrangement of words, and words are the only possible medium of thought.

You must never wait for inspiration before you write. It isn't that inspiration doesn't exist, but it comes only with writing. I've never met any writer who waited for inspiration. One begins to write a novel with a conscious effort, by using what I'll term—regardless of physiological accuracy—the front part of the brain.

And here I contradict myself. For it isn't possible to write about the act of creation without contradicting oneself at some stage. And if you have the capacity to create you'll understand this. There must be a moment of stillness for the picture to emerge. You must see some part of the novel. It will be only a small part and it will be from any point in the novel. With me it's always the end of the novel. It isn't an idea which visits me, because that's abstract. It's a picture of something happening to somebody. It can be based on something which has happened to me or to someone else or which I've been told happened to someone else. Not that it's necessary even to be aware of its origin; it's enough that one has the picture.

But the picture won't come unless the conscious decision to write the novel is taken and a date set to begin it. And here I become even more drearily down-to-earth. You must now draw up a timetable and stick to it. When you'll write and what rate you'll write at are a matter of individual capacity and circumstance, but I suggest that three two-hourly sessions a week are quite enough. It is essential that you record the number of words written each session. This has a valuable psychological effect: Whether you're pleased with what you've written or not, you have before you the proof that you're achieving something, that you actually are working. What prevents most first novels from being written is the sheer magnitude of the task, the writer's feeling that such a huge achievement isn't within the realm of possibility. The record of a steadily growing number of words dispels this feeling.

The amount of words which you set yourself to produce each session is for you to decide, though I would suggest a minimum of three hundred and fifty. All that matters is to get the words down regardless of what you feel like. Unless you're very fortunate, you won't always feel irresistibly impelled to write. And tormenting problems and apparently irrecoverable disasters come to us all. But you must write the requisite number of words at the set time even if you're half-mad with worry or your heart is breaking. There is a bonus, too: Once the writing is under way, everything else disappears from the mind. But this only happens if one's purpose is to write; it won't happen if one's purpose is to forget one's troubles. The primary purpose of writing is not therapeutic.

That ends the most important part of this book. If you disregard it, there's no point in reading on. If you remember it, if you act upon my advice, then everything you need will come to you. A writer is a person who writes; a writer is a person who counts words. Even now, after having been a professional writer since 1957, I have to remind myself of this every day. With part of me I always want merely to dream, to wait to be descended upon, to be possessed and used. I have never met any professional writer who wasn't haunted by this myth. I have never met any professional writer who didn't work set hours.

There are as many working methods as there are writers. Some use a typewriter, some a pen, some dictate—it's a waste of time to particularize further, and positively harmful to recommend any method. I personally write in longhand in stiff-backed exercise books; there is the advantage of being able to work anywhere, but the disadvantage of not producing a copy as I write, and of having to find a typist. I should recommend that you learn how to type and that you buy yourself a typewriter. Whether you actually write your novel on the typewriter or not, it is always preferable to type the manuscript for submission to the publisher yourself.

I shan't discuss the question of where to write, since virtually no spare-time writer has much choice. It hardly need be said that solitude and quiet are highly desirable, but the lack of them is no barrier to writing. I wrote much of *Room at the Top* as it now stands in a hospital bed with people constantly going and coming around me. The will to work builds all the seclusion that one needs. You can't wait until circumstances are ideal, though this doesn't mean that you mustn't strive to get the ideal circumstances for yourself.

But remember that it means sacrifice—of pleasure, of rest, of friendship, even of love. Most people accept that to sit on a committee, to learn to play a musical instrument, to learn one's lines for a play, require a definite expenditure of time and absence from the family circle. It's only writing which is supposed to be the result of some magic process, which isn't to be taken seriously. For a girl to stay in to wash her hair would be a perfectly acceptable excuse for refusing an invitation; for her to stay in to write wouldn't. A price has to be paid for everything you want; the price for writing in your spare time is the highest of all.

About the ways in which a novel can be created, as distinct from the physical methods of writing, I propose to say very little. Instead I suggest that you read the *Paris Review* series on writers at work. It's worth reading as an example of what the interview should be, worth reading to confirm your vocation—worth reading, perhaps, because it might even prove to you that you haven't a vocation, that the price is too high.

I do not advise that you treat the series as a consumer's guide, debating with yourself which is the best method. This debate can protract itself and become a substitute for writing. The excuse for abandoning the novel halfway can be that you've chosen the wrong method. I shall only recommend one method. Its disadvantages are unimportant. Its outstanding advantage is that it compels you to finish the novel quickly.

What happens in the novel you don't know until you finish it. A novel isn't a kernel of story with a softer substance of narrative around it; it's the same consistency all the way through. You need some sort of guideline, some rough idea of where you're going; you don't need, and shouldn't attempt, a complete scaffolding. You will be given a scene, a small part of the whole. It may be imagined, it may be what you've personally seen, it may be a scrap of conversation or the look on someone's face. But upon that foundation you can construct, quite consciously, the briefest of synopses. Five hundred words is enough. Making it longer and more and more elaborate can become an occupation in itself. It can be a fascinating one, but it'll get you no nearer finishing the novel.

You don't need to know anything about your characters. They will reveal themselves in their actions. But it will save you trouble later if at this stage you take their surnames not, as some writers suggest, from the telephone directory but from the gazetteer. Go through the gazetteer, preferably the *Times Gazetteer of the World*, and pick out thirty or so plausible-sounding names to be used as surnames. Choose them also according to nationality of your characters, if that is known to you. I'll go into the question of names, and libel in general, shortly; in the meantime, to have a pool of names saves holding up the narrative.

You then begin the first draft. As Hemingway said, all that matters about this is to finish it. You must set yourself a target of at least sixty thousand words, you must write the maximum amount of words possible each session, you mustn't revise, you mustn't go back, you mustn't check. You must never miss a session; if you do, you interrupt the flow. It isn't impossible to resume it, but it'll slow you down for a while. If you forget a character's name or the colour of his eyes, if you feel that more detail is needed about anyone or anything, make a note in the margin to that effect. The more quickly you write, the better. It's of no consequence if the story doesn't seem to hang together, and though you should try to fill out the story as much as you can, it's of no consequence what you leave out.

There are only three technical points to bear in mind. You must have at least twenty chapters, each must end with a hook to draw you on into the next chapter, and you must end with a bang. There must be nothing vague about the end of the novel. If in doubt about the chapter ending, let it be as improbable and melodramatic as you like, provided only you don't stop writing to think about it. When you reach the end

21

of the novel, it is permissible to slow down and to take some pains. You will, in fact, discover that even if you didn't know the end before you began, you'll know it long before you finish.

When the first draft is finished, you're given your first reward, a sense of accomplishment. You wouldn't be given it for the most perfect synopsis. However rough or disjointed, you've produced a narrative, something which you can work upon. You have proved to yourself that you don't need to wait for inspiration. You have proved to yourself that you have the staying power necessary to write a novel. And you have begun to uncover the real novel, the novel which will be published. There is no way of uncovering it except by this first unremitting hard labour.

At the next stage comes the summary, a condensed version of the story. You shouldn't bother about counting the words produced each session: All that matters is to keep on writing. At this stage you are thinking the story through; but you must think in writing, not in your head. Don't stop writing in order to think—what use is an unrecorded idea?

The best method is to write the summary of the novel again and again until you've got a credible story. The sorting out of your ideas comes with each succeeding draft. If you write quickly—ideally producing a summary each session—this will be reflected in the finished novel. The narrative will have an organic unity; it won't be a bundle of loosely linked episodes. And it will flow compulsively; it won't stop and start, run and stagger. It isn't that the pace of a novel should always be the same, but it should only be varied by design.

You mustn't, however, consider these matters too closely. You mustn't attempt to analyze your own creative processes. You mustn't think in the abstract. You mustn't ask yourself if your story has unity and pace, only if it's a good story. Don't, I need hardly say, tell it to anyone; but imagine yourself telling it to someone. You're telling it to them about people in real life, you've just heard the real truth about them, the scandalous and shocking inside story, and you can't wait to pass it on.

I suggest that this story shouldn't be any more than two thousand words. To write it out half-a-dozen times is quite enough. The danger with planning is that it can become a substitute for writing the novel. So can research. The less the better, and none at all is preferable. It isn't that it doesn't matter about your getting details of fact absolutely right; but with the first novel you should know the facts before you start. The process which began with the first draft should not be interrupted for any longer than is strictly necessary. You can't have a blueprint of a novel because its material is animate and unpredictable, not inanimate and measurable.

You can be exact in only one particular, that of length: Sixty thousand words should be the minimum, one hundred thousand the maximum. First novels considerably under and over these figures have been accepted, but these were the exceptions. It is possible for a first novel of publishable standard to be rejected for reasons of length alone. What length a novel ought to be is irrelevant. You're writing this novel to be published, and it's incredibly stupid to reduce your chances of publication simply to play the role of dedicated artist. After all, it isn't as if good novels haven't been written within these lengths.

At this point the story should be reduced to synopsis form and divided into at least twenty chapters. You must work out when each event or sequence of events takes place; you should be exact to the hour, not only the date. And you must always bear in mind the seasons, the working day, the weekend, the holidays, school terms, the length of time it takes for a woman to know she's pregnant, and so on. All of these things have their bearing on the story. If you don't work them out properly now, you'll have trouble later on; the further you've gone into the narrative, the more difficult it will be to put it right. The more the synopsis is reduced, the better. For this is only a guide. No matter how well it hangs together, it mustn't be too binding.

Simultaneously, you should decide the actual period of the story. You should know when it's all happening. The reader should know too. You don't have to quote newspaper headlines regularly or have your characters argue at length about the great issues of the day, nor should you yourself add any historical notes. The majority of people, in this country at least, are only interested in their own lives, and the great issues of the day leave them cold. They only hope to get through life with the minimum of trouble and the maximum of pleasure. This may be deplorable, but it isn't the novelist's job to deplore it.

There can be no rules about the ideal length of time for the action of the novel to cover, but a year should be your limit. There is something stagey and unreal about long leaps in time in a novel of under one hundred thousand words: All that it boils down to is the dreary commonplace that the passing of the years makes a difference to us all. Your aim should be to show us your characters during a period when suddenly, almost despite themselves, events start to move; everything they do and say is significant.

A straightforward passage in time with no flashbacks is best. It is absolutely legitimate for your characters to remember what happened in the past; they'd be very odd if they didn't. But they should talk about or think about it; it mustn't be presented in the same way as the main action of the novel. And it should be kept brief; go into the past for much over five hundred words and the story comes to a dead stop. This isn't to denigrate the device of the flashback, but simply to advise against its use in a first novel.

Next it's necessary to get a dreary chore out of the way. This has nothing to do with creation, but everything to do with self-preservation. No one except you can do it. It can't be left

24

to a lawyer; the most that he can do is to check that you haven't used the name of any real person or place or organization or manufactured object in such a way that an action for libel could ensue. There is no need to be nervous about this. Whenever you use a real name, simply don't be defamatory. A character can say that he doesn't like the smell of a certain brand of soap, for instance; that's a question of taste. If he says that it causes dermatitis, he's in deep trouble. (Incidentally, remember that brand names should be capitalized: Brylcreem, Kodak, Thermos, etc.)

I shall not give here a full definition of the law of libel; it is essential that you go to the nearest library and look it up for yourself. I shall only say that a libel is a statement which damages a person's reputation. If one of your characters has the name of a real person—and if what you say about the behaviour of that character is libellous, then you can be sued for libel. Just to make it more difficult, a positively sympathetic portrayal of a character would, under some circumstances, be held to be libellous. If, for instance, you portrayed a financier as fundamentally kindhearted, only waiting for the chance to sack his hatchet men and forgive all his debtors, then a financier who could be identified as that character might well maintain that you had damaged his reputation. It is safest not to use real names. The fact that you may not know of the existence of the owner of the real name is no defence; to quote the old saying, what matters is not who is aimed at, but who is hit.

Outside of checking every electors list in the United Kingdom—and these lists are for obvious reasons never entirely complete or up to date—the only precaution which you can take against using real names is to check the list of your characters' names which you've selected from the gazetteer against the relevant phone and professional directories. Wherever they live, you should always check the London directory. If their profession doesn't have a directory and they're employed by a known firm or organization, write to their personnel director. Check the names of fictitious firms against directories like *Kelly's Merchants Manufacturers and Shippers*. In short, check all fictitious names by whatever means are available and keep a record of this.

Despite all this you may still have used a real name. But if, according to the definition of the Defamation Act, 1952, you have used that name innocently and have taken all reasonable precautions, then an offer of an apology and the publication of a correction bars further proceedings if accepted and is a defence if not accepted. In effect, if you have taken these precautions and if you haven't been so insanely reckless as to have had a real person in mind, then you're fairly safe. Most people who bring libel actions are interested in money, not apologies.

It is imperative, however, to note that no amount of checking will save you if you recognizably portray a real person. If, to choose the only safe example possible, you depict in your novel a novelist instantly recognizable as John Braine who, shall we say, has blackmailed someone into ghosting all his novels for him, unpaid, then I shall sue you for libel and be awarded enormous damages. It won't save you if no human being at any time has had the same name as your character.

It's true, of course, that many novelists—Huxley, Wells, and Maugham, to name only three—have used real people, and not used them kindly either. But they knew that those people were highly unlikely to sue them, were indeed in some cases flattered at being chosen as models. In any case, what other novelists have got away with is no defence. Your rule must be not to use recognizable real people, to take precautions against using real names and never even to contemplate making your novel the means of repaying grudges or, for that matter, exposing wrongdoing.

It shouldn't be necessary for me to dwell at such length

over this matter. It should be possible for the names to be chosen according to how they fit your characters, as indeed they were in the last century. But *should be* isn't *is*. A successful action against you for libel could easily mean financial ruin and the withdrawal of your novel. This chore must not be avoided. There are, after all, a great many names in a comprehensive gazetteer. And for minor characters or characters who are presented in, so to speak, a neutral way, common names can be used.

Incidentally, it is often the most talented who are the most careless about this matter of libel. One example sticks in my mind; I shall not name it because in connection with libel the least said the better. It was the sequel to a brilliant first novel, a novel which I have read and reread with increasing pleasure and admiration and from which I, and others of my generation, have learned much of our craft. The second novel was suppressed on grounds of libel and now there's a gap in the twentieth-century novel which never can be filled. The suppression of a good novel seems to me not far short of tragedy. Don't let it happen to you: Perform the chore at this stage, and then libel can be put out of your mind once and for all.

(The foregoing applies to English law. The position in the U.S.A. is very different. The principles of U.S. libel law are very much the same as in England, and novelists have been sued for libel and have paid damages. But in practice the novelist in the U.S.A. has a great deal more freedom. If he didn't have, then novelists like Harold Robbins and Mario Puzo would be ruined men. In fact, one of the reasons for Robbins's and Puzo's success is that their characters can be identified with real people. Naturally, these are celebrities. The public always wants the lowdown on people like Frank Sinatra and Dean Martin and Howard Hughes and Lana Turner—a novel offers them the real lowdown, the story that even the U.S. newspapers wouldn't dare to print.

27

John Braine

Or, rather, it appears to; fiction is *skilfully* mixed with fact. And the reader has the delicious sensation of being on the inside, of being the only one to see through the image so expensively fabricated by the P.R. machine. He isn't, of course; but reading is essentially a solitary occupation, and he has the illusion that he is. It's a labour-saving way of creating character and a great help to sales; it doesn't to me have much to do with the sort of novel I personally want to write. It isn't that good novelists haven't used real people as models; Monroe Stahr in Scott Fitzgerald's *The Last Tycoon* is an obvious instance. But Stahr was himself, not Irving Thalberg. Fitzgerald went forward from Thalberg; it's Stahr about whom we want to know. Stahr is alive and Thalberg is dead, merely a Hollywood producer, of any consequence only to students of the cinema. What must be noted is that if *The Last Tycoon* had been published in Thalberg's lifetime, and if U.S. libel law had been identical with English libel law, I doubt whether Thalberg could or would have sued.

So I have let the section on libel stand. If you act under the assumption that the U.S. libel law is as strict as British libel law you'll not only be completely safe but, which is more important, you'll write better novels. If you decide to fictionalize celebrities, you're reasonably safe to do so in the U.S., and it can be very profitable. I don't especially condemn it, because I don't believe that the celebrities concerned are hurt by it—on the contrary, I believe that they're flattered. (But I don't intend to advise you on how to write this—or any—kind of best-seller.)

There remain now only two tasks before the actual writing of the second draft. Again, the more quickly they're accomplished the better. You must compile the briefest possible biographical notes on your characters—age, physical appearance, occupation, income, education, war service if any, marital state, ages of children if any, and so on. You must confine yourself to what is strictly essential. Their age is the most important detail of all; vagueness about it can lead to confusion and wasted effort later on.

This advice I got from Miss Pamela Hansford Johnson. When I consider it, I see one of the main reasons for the solidity and precision of her work. It isn't important whether you use all the details about your characters; it is vital for them to be there. A novel, Ernest Hemingway said, is like an iceberg, two-thirds of it below the surface. You can, of course, invent only the details of character which you need for the purposes of the story. But in that case the characters will only exist for the purposes of the story. They won't move the story, the story will move them.

These potted biographies, like the synopsis itself, must not be regarded as binding. The story will change the characters—or, rather, make you see them clearly. You can't see them as they really are until you see them in action. You don't know how they will develop, play a greater or a lesser part in the story. If they are to be credible as human beings, their behaviour shouldn't be predictable.

The second task is to establish the geography of the novel. As much effort must be expended in making the places in your novel real as in making the people real. It isn't enough to wheel a sort of stage set into place. How much or how little the places in which we live affect us is infinitely variable according to person and circumstance. What isn't variable is the actual physical existence of these places. If we use real places, there's no problem: We use maps and street plans. If fictitious, we draw our own. The degree of detail depends upon our skill and the requirements of the story; what is important is that we should always know exactly where everything is happening.

It should go without saying that you should write the second draft with the synopsis and the potted biographies and the maps and street plans beside you. I personally keep them in the same stiff-backed exercise book which I also use for making notes. In the exercise books I use for the actual second draft, I use only one side of each page, leaving one clear for insertions and amendments. This is, of course, simply what suits me personally; but the matter is worth some thought. Whether you use longhand or a typewriter, you need to keep all your work together, to have it in easily portable form, and to be able instantly to find any part of it you may need. For you have no time to waste.

. So much for the tasks which are carried out by your conscious mind, by the front half of the brain. There comes next an exploration. You may be one of the fortunate people for whom it isn't necessary. You may have made the journey at some point in the first draft. Instantaneously you may have made it even before the first draft, as soon as you had hit upon the theme of the novel.

But what is more likely is that you simply won't be able to begin the second draft. What you are writing *about* presents no problem. You've done all the groundwork, you've done all your chores. The block of stone is, as it were, very roughly hewn out in final shape. Now comes the sculpture, the manuscript which you'll send to a publisher. You can't go on planning and note-taking for ever. In fact, I believe that for most of us—certainly for me—there comes a stage when further work on any preliminary to the final draft is positively harmful. It seems professional to make one's synopsis fuller and fuller, to add detail after detail to the potted biographies, to make the maps and street plans more and more elaborate, but it couldn't be more amateurish. A professional novelist writes novels for publication.

This is the first bad moment. There will be others, but none as bad as this. What you must on no account do is to wait for inspiration. Rescue is not going to arrive from anyone but yourself. So far I have spoken of writing as I would speak of any other kind of work. So in one sense it is. In another it isn't. It's an art. The ability to write is a gift; there have been some very fancy explanations of why some should have the gift and not others, but never yet a satisfactory one.

The greatest danger is that at this moment you may put the novel aside, telling yourself that you've been working too hard, that you can't see the wood for the trees, that maybe you should begin again. I have no way of proving it, but I believe that, once put aside, the novel is never taken up again.

The bad moment will never be so bad with future novels. You will know then that you've survived it. But this is your first encounter with the dragon, the first time you've met a problem which can't be solved by the conscious will alone.

Whenever you're in deep trouble—and this doesn't only apply to writing—the first thing to do is to gather all the information you can about the trouble. Until you know exactly what it is, you can't do anything about it. There isn't very much information available on this particular trouble; what is available isn't reliable since some writers make it seem even worse than it is and others play it down, according to whether their public presence is the sensitive tormented artist or the serenely matter-of-fact professional.

There is, of course, some encouragement to be derived from the fact that other writers have been in the same position. But the only clear picture I've ever come across is in Norman Podhoretz's autobiography, *Making It*:

Writing is among the most mysterious of human activities. No one, least of all the psychoanalysts, knows the laws by which it moves or refuses to move. . . . The poem, the story, the essay, and even . . . a book review . . . is already there . . . before a word is ever put to paper; and the act of writing is the act of finding the magical key that will unlock the floodgates and let the flow begin. . . .

31

It is not within the power of his will to summon it forth if it refuses to come; nor is he capable of resisting it long when it starts to demand release. . . .

But if the act of writing cannot be controlled by the will, it can be controlled by that magical key of which I have already spoken. The key, I believe, is literally a key in that it is musical . . . it is the tone of voice, the only tone of voice, in which this particular piece of writing will permit itself to be written. . . . Yet the unconscious, or the Muse, or whatever it is, often exacts a sacrifice from the writer before it will allow him to hit upon the right tone, the key. . . .[2]

This is exactly how it is. You don't come to a dead stop because you don't know what to write about. You're well aware of what you're going to write about. You come to a dead stop because you haven't yet hit upon the way to write it. It isn't a question of style, of the way in which you arrange words, it isn't a question of construction. The phrase to hang on to is *the tone of voice*. You can't put it into any other words; you must on no account use any other words to describe it.

Podhoretz speaks of a sacrifice which often has to be made. I don't think that this need be very great with your first novel. What is asked is only time and thought. In this instance, you have to think before you write. You have to be absolutely honest with yourself about what tone of voice comes naturally to you. It won't necessarily be the tone of voice of the novelist whom you most admire. The clothes which look splendid on someone else will rarely look splendid on you. Indeed, the most glaring fault of the majority of first novels is that a tone of voice has been chosen which doesn't suit their authors; by a heroic act of will the novels have been finished, but they've been written against the grain, there is no flow of life.

Sit quietly and think, and think at every opportunity. There must be no panic and no hurry. There is no deadline, and you're not dependent upon writing for your daily bread. Put all generalizations out of your head. Don't think in the abstract. See your characters as real people and visualize how they'll meet the reader. Don't think about the plot of the novel; think about specific situations. Aim at making pictures, not notes. Relax and let your mind go free. When the right tone of voice comes, you'll recognize it. Don't begin until then. And only worry about the first paragraph. Don't worry about what comes after.

Very often you'll find that you write very slowly at the beginning of the second draft. Again, there must be no panic. It isn't simply that you must find the right tone of voice; you must establish yourself in it. But I lay down no hard-and-fast rule about what your rate of production should be. With the first draft all that matters is writing the maximum number of words; with the second draft all that matters is putting in the maximum amount of time. Everything must be got exactly right, no detail must be skimped, nothing must be left to be revised later.

Under no circumstances should you break off work at this stage for any appreciable period. It won't, as for example Georges Simenon says, be impossible for you to start again from where you left off; but it will be extremely difficult. Time will have to be expended in going back into the story again, in finding its proper rhythm. And if you don't expend the time, it will show in the novel: There'll be a yawning gap.

The second bad moment, for me, comes after the first five thousand words, when it doesn't seem possible that I can write another seventy-five thousand. There is nothing that can be done except to keep on and not to hurry. If you're uncertain about even one sentence, write it out again and again until you get it right. It is always preferable to do this separately; the second draft itself should be a reasonably fair

33

copy. If it isn't, if half of it is crossed out, then you can't possibly count the number of words accurately.

I'm well aware that my preoccupation with the number of words actually written may seem absurd, unconnected with the creation of literature, even a trifle sordid. But a real writer, as opposed to someone who is simply attracted by the idea of being a writer, counts words. And the words you're counting now are publishable words—all of the best, as Arnold Bennett used to say.

So much for the bad moments; once you've found the right tone of voice, there may not be any at all, or they may not last very long. For me the first good moment, the real breakthrough, comes when I look at a passage or a sentence and honestly admire it. This seems conceited, but let it stand; conceit has nothing to do with it, for it's as if someone else had written it. The novel then has taken over. It has its own life outside you. In a sense it's writing itself. You'll know when this moment comes. You may have written much else of equal merit; that is irrelevant. You can't keep stopping to pat yourself on the back; but there will always be at least this one pat on the back to tell you you're going in the right direction.

One thing remains to be said about the second draft: When you're approaching the end, don't be tempted to hurry. It always shows. It is a good general rule to slow down toward the end, and if you've set yourself a deadline, deliberately to extend it.

About the preparation of the manuscript for sending to a publisher, I'll say very little. All that the publisher requires is a legible and adequately protected typescript with adequate margins. You'll find all the information you require on this in publications like *The Writers' and Artists' Year Book*.[3]

Which publisher to send it to is another matter. There is no genuinely comprehensive publishers' guide, and because of the laws of libel, there can never be one. A good rule is to try the best and the biggest first, then work your way down. Don't try the smallest first. You should, of course, know which is the best and the biggest, but if you don't, then a rapid inspection of the nearest library or bookshop will tell you. All this is a matter of common sense.

So, too, ought to be the question of employing a literary agent. The time to consider this is when—and only when—your novel has been accepted and before you sign the contract.* An agent isn't a literary adviser. He is not interested in unsolicited manuscripts. His function is to obtain for you the best possible terms for your work and to deal with all the business side of it. His payment for this is 10 percent of your payment. You don't have written contracts with literary agents and they don't charge you anything beyond their 10 percent (which is, incidentally, a legitimate tax deduction). As

*David Higham, my friend and British agent since 1951, writes, "You are wrong, so far as we are concerned at any rate, in saying that we don't want unsolicited manuscripts. We do, even though nine out of ten are no good. Also, without ourselves personally (or most of us) claiming any kind of judgement of literary merit, we do employ reasonably skilful readers who are able to tackle any type of novel: and we do have one thing to offer authors at this very early stage—a knowledge of the *kind* of publisher who is likely to do best for a particular kind of book. I think your ready reckoner that says go to the largest and then on down as it were isn't really very sound market advice to an author. It is easy to offer to, well, say, Hodder, who fulfil your top qualifications as stated, a novel which would be far better on Secker's list who don't—and so forth.

"Actually, I think that to have an agent from the very start is of great value to an author. The agent will get better terms than you will get direct and he will have more chance of getting those terms if the publisher hasn't made an offer direct to the author before he knows an agent is involved. One discusses these things with publishers and they make a proposal to an agent which is financially considerably better, both as to terms, rights and conditions, than they would make direct."

Strangely enough, the general feeling among U.S. publishers is identical with this. They much prefer to deal through agents.

with publishers, go for the best and biggest. The best in this instance means the longest established.

Have nothing to do with any agent who asks you for a fee or to sign a contract. I'm not going to advise you against any publisher who asks you for money since I'm not writing for half-wits.

As soon as you've finished the novel, give yourself one working week off, then spend the next three weeks planning your second novel. You should have finished at least the first draft before your first novel is published. And it should be absolutely different from the first. Even though the period between acceptance and publication can be these days as long as nine months (unlike the leisured days before the war, when the average was three months), the time can all too easily slip by in fiddling with the manuscript of the first and, when that's no longer possible, in daydreaming about the golden future. There are always excuses for even the full-time writer not to write—there are even more for the part-time writer.

TWO: Always write from experience

Always write from experience. Your own experience is absolutely unique. If you're going to be heard out of all those thousands of voices, if your name is going to mean something out of all those thousands of names, it will only be because you've presented your own experience truthfully.

It doesn't matter how limited your experience has been. (It is hardly possible for it to have been more limited than mine.) If you've lived in the same house all your life, if you've had the same dull routine job ever since leaving school, if nothing remarkable has ever happened to you, if you have never even had such basic experiences as making love or seeing someone close to you die, you still have the material for a thousand novels. Where you live doesn't matter. Your class and your income and your colour and your education don't matter. It doesn't matter what you look like. It doesn't matter about your health. It doesn't matter about your disabilities: To quote only one example, Christy Brown, a housebound cripple in a Dublin slum, with no formal education whatever, wrote a successful first novel.

In fact, too exciting a life, too many adventures, too much travel, too much of the world of action, are positively a handicap to the novelist. The danger is that he becomes too much the participant, not enough the observer. Writers like Tolstoy and Hemingway are the exceptions to the rule. I agree that war is a valuable experience for the writer, but it isn't an indispensable one. More good writers haven't had it than have had it. The qualities which make a good writer are precisely those which lessen a soldier's chance of survival.

A writer must watch for the relevant detail, the detail which will epitomize the whole event. Epitomize it, that is, for the reader who is always there with him. From the military point of view the detail may be absolutely irrelevant. Indeed, even a second spent in finding the right word for the colour of the enemy's uniform, the expressions of their faces as they advance, the smells in the trench around one, may be fatal. The predominant feeling of the novelist is that everything is too much for him, that too many impressions are pouring in upon him. He sees, as Arnold Bennett said, like a child or an idiot, as if for the first time. The camera registers everything within its range of vision; afterwards comes the editing. But the soldier has to edit as he goes along: The information he needs has to be gathered instantaneously.

The same applies to big-game hunting, surgery, flying, and so on. It isn't that one couldn't be an adept at these and at the same time be a good novelist, but I don't think that it happens very often. I would establish it as a general principle that the more you give to your job, the less you have to give to your writing. On the other hand, it's an illusion that demanding jobs are necessarily well-paid or undemanding jobs ill-paid. The ideal would be to have a reasonably remunerative and interesting job, preferably unconnected with literature—doctor or lawyer or engineer, for example—and then have a late vocation for the novel. But it would be a great mistake to regard one's job merely as a means of earning the absolute necessities of life. You may as well be a director as an ordinary clerk: The director knows what life at the clerk's level is like, but the clerk doesn't know about life at the director's level. I don't recommend the Bohemian life—to use an old-fashioned phrase—because it imperceptibly puts one out of touch with life as the majority lives it. And too much of the company of one's fellow writers can lead to sterility. As John Dos Passos said, writers are like fleas, critters which get little nourishment from one another. Occasionally to talk shop is stimulating and helps rid one of the sense of isolation which is the burden of the writer; but to talk shop too often, to think of oneself as being that wonderful and superior creature, a *writer*, separates one from one's material.

On the whole, it's best not to talk about being a writer, not to look and behave as one imagines a writer should behave, but to conform outwardly with the society in which one lives. And—though this is a counsel of perfection—it's better to listen than to speak, to be unnoticed rather than noticed, to observe rather than be involved. It is better, too, right from the first never to become associated with any political party or any cause, no matter how good. It is better, too, never to write letters to the papers, no matter how strongly one may feel. Let everything go into your writing; let your novel be the receptacle for all that you think and feel. I don't, of course, mean that your novel should express your political beliefs; for instance, that you should have one of your characters write the letter to the paper on whatever is making you burn with emotion. I mean that if you don't speak at a public meeting, don't carry a banner in a demo, don't write a letter to the papers, the emotion itself will find its way into your novel. Don't let your emotions be frittered away on what is ephemeral.

The greatest objection to the writer's taking sides is that sooner or later he'll be led into seeing human beings in black-and-white terms. The people on the other side, indeed, won't be quite human to him. This is not to say that good and evil don't exist, only that they have nothing to do with politics. Once it would have been necessary in a book like this to remind you that the drunken navvy lying in a pool of vomit in Wapping on a Saturday night is a human being; now it's necessary to remind you that the Bermuda-tanned stock-broker sipping champagne in his mansion in Virginia Water is a human being.

It isn't your job to pass judgement on anyone, much less on society. It isn't your job to say what *should* be, only what *is*. No person, no place, no object, no event is dull or boring or commonplace. Everything is to be remembered, everything is to be used. I believe that a true novelist is perpetually fascinated by the life around him, grows to love it even though he may ardently desire to get away from it. His experience isn't really his own life—I believe also that a true novelist doesn't in the proper sense have any life of his own—but a non-stop record of actuality. Even when he's directly involved, he has the feeling that somehow he isn't deciding his words and actions personally. Unreality is part of it too. There is no order or form or purpose in the non-stop record.

How fully it should be noted down or whether it should be noted down at all is a matter of personal choice. I have myself kept a diary since I was twenty, but I've never consulted it for use in my novels. To keep a notebook or a repository of useful material would be unnatural to me. It isn't that I don't ever record personal experiences or ideas for future novels in my diaries; but I never go back to them. If I do use them, there isn't any need to; I remember because I've written them down. But most often I don't make notes; I'll remember what I need to remember.

What must be held fast to, what I can't repeat too often, is the fact that what isn't written from experience is worthless. You must never write about what you don't know. Not to use the unique material which you have in your possession is a kind of suicide. It is never that there isn't enough. For by experience I don't mean only direct personal experience. What you have seen or heard of happening to someone else is personal experience. For example, all Joe Lampton's memories of his time in the R.A.F. are others' memories, not mine. I didn't write them down when I was told them; I remembered them when I needed them. I didn't have much option but to use others' memories; my own wartime experiences were a singularly uneventful nine months in the Navy, mostly spent in training. But the source of the material doesn't matter, only the use you make of it.

There is more to the use of personal experience than a simple transfer; fiction is more than reportage. The experience is transmuted when given to your character, may have more or less significance than it had to its original participant. Your instincts will inform you when you hit upon something valuable; it might even be a newspaper story or a scene in a film or TV newsreel. There is always a feeling of pure gloating joy, irrespective of what horror or distress may be inseparable from the happening; the fact that you do feel joy is the main reason for good novelists not being quite human.

Your own direct experience is rarely of much use as material at the time; you're too involved. There's always a period needed to digest it, to get it into perspective; with me it's at least five years. I don't mean by experience simple observation of what's happening around you, but any event or series of events which brings out some positive reaction. Experience has the shape of drama. But you aren't a dramatic critic, rushing off immediately after the last curtain descends to write your notice, the copyboy standing at your shoulders to seize each completed page.

To write a novel is, above all, to remember. You must learn to be quiet, to compose yourself, to let the memories enter. Apart from the time which you spend writing, you must have quiet periods, during which you can empty your mind of the day's events, shut off the present. Quiet places aren't necessary. Even solitude isn't necessary. You only need time. Don't be frightened of even the most unpleasant memories;

41

bring them out and you cease to be frightened. There must be no locked cupboards, no bolted doors, in the novelist's mind: you need all that is there from which to select. It is what has hurt you that is the most valuable of all. Write about it and it will hurt you no more.

I didn't really believe this when I first came across it, in slightly different words, in Somerset Maugham's autobiography; not until I'd written my first novel did I find out the truth of it. But writing isn't therapy; on the contrary, it twists and distorts the psyche. If the experience has lost its power to hurt you, it doesn't necessarily mean that you're a better person. The hurtful experience is what is best for the novel, what makes it authentic and alive and not mere fabrication.

You must set aside time to remember and time in which to write and read; on top of that, unless you're the one in a million with an independent income, you've a living to earn. I'm aware that it's a counsel of perfection, but try not to get married or permanently entangled before your novel is finished. An accepted novel means that your writing can be taken seriously, as seriously as any of the recognized claims on your spare time. But, no matter how intelligent the other person in the case may be, they won't take kindly to being deprived of your company every evening or even every other evening for an unfinished novel. You should accept that for the majority of people, to have someone near to them actually publish a book isn't seen as being within the bounds of possibility.

There are, of course, several other arguments against marriage. They're so obvious that I'm not going to put them down. I shall only say that to be restricted in any way, not to be free to go anywhere and do anything, and to be forced to think seriously about money, can be fatal to your novel. It might even lead you into thinking of your novel as the means of solving all your financial problems, which will in turn lead you to telling your wife or husband that you're writing it for their sake. Write for money, and you'll get no money. Tell a lie about your work, and you'll pay for it. For you don't produce any work of art for anybody's sake but your own, no matter how much you love the other person. Come to that, you don't even produce it for your own sake, but for its own.

I cannot qualify my statements about marriage for the writer because I can't change the nature of time. Nor can I change the nature of human relationships. The claims of your first novel and the claims of your partner cannot be reconciled; the only way of doing it would be for you to stay at home and let them go out to work. (And there, when I look at it, is not only a qualification but a sensible and practical one.)

I follow with another statement which won't be easy for the majority to accept. A first novel shouldn't be written much before the age of thirty.

For the danger is that a young writer tends to be wasteful with his material, to cram everything in that has happened to him up to the time of writing. In one sense he gives the reader full value—the novel is overflowing with material. All the experiences which excite him are here. In another sense he cheats the reader, for the reader wants a novel, not a fictionalized autobiography. And since there is too much material, most of it is treated skimpily. The meat has, as it were, been crammed in raw. The material of the book hasn't been handled properly, most of it has been wasted. It isn't until maturity that one learns to be economical with one's material, to have a positive horror of autobiography.

In fact, an early success is possibly the worst thing that can happen to a young novelist. He's confirmed in his bad habits, he continues to be autobiographical, until he reaches the final stage of writing about the novel he is writing. To wait until maturity—which may indeed come before thirty—means not only that one adds to one's store of experience, but that there's time to learn one's craft. And the craft of the novel shouldn't be learned upon the novel itself but in other forms. There is an advantage here, too, in that some reputation may be acquired in these other forms. And certainly self-confidence can be acquired; to have one's name in print can help one through the bad moments.

And, curiously enough, the more one has been published, the less one is tempted to commit the ultimate sin of writing a novel about a novelist.

The objection to this is that the novel becomes like the old box of Quaker Oats with an oval insert showing a Quaker holding up a box of Quaker Oats on which was discernible an oval insert on which, I used to think as a child, must have been another picture of a Quaker. . . . When did it stop? When did we get to the oats? When, in a novel about a novelist writing a novel about a novelist, do we get to the novel? And if the novel the hero is writing isn't about a novelist, why can't we have the novel instead?

This is not to say that in midcareer you may not write a novel about a novelist; you'll then have had the experience of being a novelist and will have lost all your illusions. And it isn't to say that Thomas Wolfe, for instance, with all his gigantic faults, doesn't have gigantic virtues. But I believe that Wolfe, precisely because his first novel had as its hero a writer who was closely modelled on himself, had reached a dead end. It isn't that novelists can't have tremendous egos, can't see themselves as otherwise but the centre of the universe, don't thrash about emotionally like harpooned whales—but basically they've got to write about other people; even though they can never get rid of themselves, they've got to try to. And they have to try to tell the truth. This is always difficult; about oneself it is impossible.

To write from experience, to put down on paper the world as you see it, doesn't, it must be added, guarantee you critical or commercial success, or even acceptance. Each era has its own prudery, its own set of conventions. But let me be strictly accurate: I'm referring to the middle-class minority which publishes books, writes reviews, and in general dominates the mass media. Eventually only the reading public—Virginia Woolf's *Common Reader*—matters, but before you reach them you have to penetrate the barrier set up by the minority.

Do not ever be tempted to write for this minority. Do not consider what is fashionable or what is timely. Do not attempt to discover trends and currents in fiction. If a publisher suggests rewriting or considerable revision, consider his reasons. If they're technical, it's worth taking notice of them. If they're political or ethical, try another publisher. And always bear in mind that though ninety-nine times out of a hundred your novel will be rejected because of sheer incompetence, the hundredth time it isn't. It boils down to this: Don't tell lies, however powerful the inducement. To tell the truth in your novel is not only the one certain way of fulfilling yourself as a writer, but also offers the best chance of being successful enough to be a full-time writer.

What depresses one the most about unpublished novels is the occasion when the writer tells the truth. For a moment there is visible the novel that could have been written, that would have been published, that would have transformed the writer's whole life. I remember once looking at a novel which was so bad that it had a weird fascination. I rather fancy that the writer had aimed at a prose style halfway between John Donne and Henry James, enlivened by a gentle allusive humour. Most of the time it was impossible to discover exactly what was happening. In amongst this was a short chapter describing the author's feelings as a child toward his father. There was no laboured metaphor, no attempt at wit. The father was seen as his small son saw him—a terrifying figure, a tyrant whom there was no pleasing. I found this

45

chapter terribly moving, and do to this day. Because he had told the truth about his own experience, I felt pity not only for the child but also for the father.

I broke my usual rule of simply returning unsolicited manuscripts with a polite note and told the author to throw the rest of the novel away and start from that chapter. It didn't matter if eventually he threw that away too; in fact, it would be a good idea to write the novel from the father's point of view. He had found the right tone of voice—though that wasn't the phrase I used—and he must go forward from there.

I won't say much about his reply, except that it was evident that I'd deeply hurt him and that he wasn't going to take the least notice of me. I haven't heard of him since, and I have never again departed from my rule of not commenting on unsolicited manuscripts. What still upsets me is that the time and effort put into what was unpublishable could have produced a publishable novel. It wasn't a question of his novel failing because he was unwilling to work. (Strangely enough, it generally is more difficult to write badly than write well.) It wasn't a question of lack of ability. The good chapter, the *true* chapter, proved that. It was that lies don't work in the novel. Whatever the attitude of the novel, however your world is viewed, it must be your own. Not your own as a public person, not your own as a Christian or an atheist or a communist or conservative, but as a private person.

A vigorous realism is the only possible way for the novel. Only through a vigorous exactitude of presentation can the essential strangeness of life be conveyed. If you don't see the surface clearly, then you'll never see what's beneath it.

You'll never be able to write a novel as long as you have the illusion that only a special kind of world is worth writing about, that the world you know is too dull and commonplace. I personally until the age of twenty-four was very much under the influence of Hemingway; I saw no likelihood of my being a novelist until I could live as Hemingway did, in the places that Hemingway lived in. In short, I wanted to be an expatriate. My material would be found in Paris, Madrid, and Havana, not the West Riding of Yorkshire. My heroines would be high-living and doomed like Catherine Ashley and Lady Brett, not the girl next door.

I wasn't so naïve as to use Hemingway locales for my stories. Instead, I attempted to transpose Hemingway characters and the Hemingway atmosphere to the West Riding. Predictably the stories were rejected. It then occurred to me, looking at the market, that there wasn't much room for short stories in any case. (The position is even worse now.)

I came to the conclusion that there was no point in writing short stories at all. What there was always room for was reportage, straightforward description of actuality. It was then that I began to be a writer, began to prepare myself to be a novelist, publishing first in *Tribune* and then in the *New Statesman*. I began with places and worked up to people. The pieces about places were also about the people who used the places: The pieces about people were also about the places they lived in. I took as much trouble with the place as with the people in both instances; both had to be equally real if the pieces were to be alive. I didn't moralize or say what should be; I was then, as now, concerned only with life as it is.

From this stage onwards I looked at the world around me exclusively. As far as I was concerned, whatever I hadn't experienced personally didn't exist. I became aware suddenly of how much material I had, material which was constantly being added to. When, some four years later, after an unsuccessful play, I began to think of writing a novel, I was determined that it shouldn't be autobiographical. There wasn't any need. There never is any need. And the way that it's done is to make your hero* someone else.

*In cases like this, "hero" should be taken to include heroine throughout.

John Braine

I don't know why so many writers, unpublished and published, should find this so hard to grasp: The novel is about other people. A first novel must always be about other people. The function of the novel isn't self-expression: It isn't to sort out your life, it isn't to change society. Above all, it isn't about you. You must use your own experience, direct and indirect, but only as the purposes of the story dictate. You must realize that you yourself don't matter. Only the work matters. You have to get rid of yourself, or at least try to.

Other people, from the point of view of the novelist, don't matter. What I have said about libel still applies, but no character can be convincing who isn't based upon a real person. *Based* upon a real person: The character you create won't have the same appearance, occupation, beliefs, way of speaking, or even necessarily be of the same sex. You start from him because something about him excites your imagination or because he is the centre of some event which excites your imagination. What emerges is a new person. I'll put it this way: If the original of any of your characters could win a libel case against you, you have failed to create a real character.

Non-writers always accuse writers of using everyone for copy. They're not actually displeased by this; everyone likes to be taken notice of, and naturally assumes that they'll be presented in the same light as they see themselves. In one sense they're wrong: Very few social occasions, for instance, can be used in their entirety, and virtually no one, even if the libel laws didn't make it so dangerous, just as they are. But if you are to be a novelist, you can waste nothing, even if to use it hurts you or someone else.

Finally, there is no formula for character creation. And it's impossible to determine whether the story emerges from the characters or the characters from the story. As I've said, my own novels start from the end: I have a picture in my mind of something happening to someone. I see him only from the outside; I don't know how he got into the situation, but I do immediately have a clear idea at least of what he looks like and how old he is. But my methods need not influence you. Of one thing I am sure: If you have your characters, it won't be long before you have your story.

THREE: Writing is seeing

Always write as if the action of your novel were taking place before your eyes on a brightly lit stage. This was the advice of Ford Madox Ford; I keep it in mind all the time when I'm working on a novel. It is the most important of my working rules.

Break all the others and with luck and talent you can still be published. The novel may not be the best you can do; it may not—however you want to measure success—be as successful as it might have been; it may lead you into a dead end. But at least it will have been published, you'll have had your chance. Break Ford Madox Ford's rule and you're finished before you've begun.

The next example of how not to write is the one quoted by Graham Greene: "He got up, went downstairs, and hailed a taxi." You should memorize this and test every sentence against it; if any has that same flat, dead quality, rewrite or cut it. You must always act on the assumption that one such sentence will ruin the whole novel. For what it gives the reader is not an impression of something happening in the real world, but of merely a string of words. He could do as well himself. In fact, he could probably do better; given the same story to tell, he'd describe how he leapt up from his chair, ran downstairs nearly breaking his neck, and how for once a taxi came by just when he wanted it, even though it was a wet day when usually none are to be had. He might even say something about the taxi driver or whether or not he was in the habit of taking taxis. He'd try to bring the sequence of events to life; for the only reason for narrating them would be that they had some special significance.

It isn't that in the novel everything must be treated with the same intensity. It isn't necessary to put in every activity of your characters. Indeed, you might well replace Ford Madox Ford's stage with a cinema screen. The rule for the novel is the same as for the film: Nothing is shown or said without a purpose. Look at each sentence of description; if nothing is seen, strike it out.

I can't tell you what to select. There are times when the only possible way to describe a character crossing a room is for you to follow each step, and times when it would be tedious to do anything except cut, to show him at one side of the room and then immediately at the other. There are times when everything within a room, down to the flyspecks on the lampshade, must be described and times when one detail would be enough. It can depend upon what's happening: If you went into a room and found a naked girl flourishing a blood-stained sword, you wouldn't look at the furniture and wallpaper.

Then there is the viewpoint: Different characters notice different things; drink and drugs and fatigue can blur the vision—or make it unnaturally clear. And whatever is on one's mind follows one everywhere; if you went into a strange room just after losing a child and saw a toy there, what else would you notice but the toy? But nothing must be left out because you can't be bothered to describe it. Whether you use it all or not, it all must be there in the mind's eye. To return to the example of the bereaved parent seeing only the toy, there is no poignancy about this selectiveness unless there's a roomful of objects to select from. And unless you as the writer see all that's in the room, you haven't seen what's in the mind of your character.

Let us consider another example of how not to write. I

made it up, but it's an absolutely typical passage from any unpublished novel and I have seen passages like it in more than one published novel.

"Tom walked over to the window. The sun had come out. He went upstairs and awakened Hilda."

This is remarkable for the number of questions it doesn't answer. How did Tom walk over to the window? Slowly? Briskly? What did he see through the window? How did he go upstairs? What did he notice on the way? Or what didn't he notice on the way? How did he awaken Hilda? If he went into the bedroom, what did she look like when she was asleep?

You don't just walk over to the window in a novel. Walking is a physical action and every physical action is revealing. And the sun doesn't simply come out in novels. *"To come out"* are three dead words. Nothing is seen. But what happens in real life is that the sun, in shades from pale yellow to bright orange, is reflected from water, from windows, from car reflectors; it brings out the colour of the grass and the trees and the flowers; it changes the colour of the sky; it makes new things look newer and old things older. What has happened isn't a general unremarkable fact, but a physical happening in the specific place you're writing about, seen by a specific person.

Going upstairs—running or walking, breathing easily or with effort—you notice wallpaper peeling or paint flaking, or note with satisfaction the new wallpaper and paintwork or do not notice anything. But just as the sun doesn't merely come out, so one doesn't merely go upstairs. There is no upstairs, there is a real staircase leading from the ground floor to the first floor in a real house, and when you go up those stairs your eyes register your surroundings.

And how does Hilda sleep? If it doesn't matter, then Hilda doesn't matter. Does she smile or frown when she's awakened? Or grunt? Is she easy or difficult to awaken? And what does she look like when she's asleep? What does Tom feel when he looks at her? Remember that sleeping people have no defences; their character is revealed. But let me qualify this. There are a few whose faces are perfectly composed, revealing nothing—is Hilda one of these?

We live in the physical world. We are not disembodied spirits. There are a few people to whom their physical surroundings are a matter of complete indifference; but even if you choose to write about these, you'll have to show just to what they're indifferent. For most of us, what we feel about the physical world, about things both natural and man-made, is part of our character. Use all your senses to apprehend the world around you, make no judgements, forget yourself, and your novel is alive. The statue is inside the stone, and unless you love the stone you won't love the statue.

John O'Hara's last novel, *The Ewings,* isn't in my opinion his best novel. I feel that he knew he hadn't got much time and was in too much of a hurry to finish it. But long after reading it, certain passages come back to my mind. If they come back at night, when I am halfway to sleep, I'm not sure whether I read them or whether I was actually there.

"How did you like my friends?" said Paul Everett.

"I like them just fine," said Bill.

"I've known them all my life, but I'd hardly say they were always friends of mine. Then one day two years ago Logan invited me to sit with them at the Round Table, and I knew I'd begun to amount to something. They just about run things in this town. It's funny, I'm the only member of Rotary that was ever invited to the Round Table. But I still go to Rotary."

"Why not?" said Bill.

"You know why not, Bill," said Everett. "But there was a time when I was lucky to get in Rotary, and I don't forget that," said Everett. "Shall we put a little mileage on the

Pierce-Arrow? You sure you don't want to take the wheel?"

"No, you drive," said Bill.

They went to the garage back of the hotel and got the car. Everett was silent for the first few minutes. "You know, for the sheer pleasure of driving you can't beat a Pierce-Arrow," he said. "It's a lot of car, mind you. It takes careful handling, and it sure eats up gas. But you expect that. I haven't had her on any long rides so far, but I get somewhere around six or seven miles to the gallon and I won't get much more, even when the car's broken in. The man from the factory told me that. He said to me, 'Don't expect a Pierce-Arrow to set any economy records, Mr. Everett.' He said it'd be the same whether I had a Packard or a Winton or any other big car. They're just not engineered to save gas and oil. . . ."⁴

I don't know why this should stick in my memory, or why it should give me such an overwhelming sense of pathos. Everett is, of course, showing off. He's telling his son-in-law, none too subtly, that he has arrived entirely through his own efforts. He has brought his son-in-law into the family; now he's bringing him into his personal circle. There are no comments, no judgements, no symbols; but behind Everett's words is the sense of the passing of time, of the fact that the younger man will one day take over.

It convinces utterly because O'Hara knew about Rotary and the Round Table and the petrol consumption of Pierce-Arrows and how a man feels about being in the position where he can afford to run a car like the Pierce-Arrow. You will note, and for the time being put it aside, that O'Hara doesn't always write in the way in which I've been recommending you to write. But when he was writing, he was there in Cleveland, Ohio, watching and listening to those two men.

Another passage which sticks in my memory is from Scott Fitzgerald's *The Great Gatsby*. Daisy, with whom Gatsby has been in love, hopelessly, since his youth, is being shown round his mansion. Nick, the narrator, is present, as a sort of chaperone, Daisy being married and Gatsby being an old-fashioned romantic.

His bedroom was the simplest room of all—except where the dresser was garnished with a toilet set of pure dull gold. Daisy took the brush with delight, and smoothed her hair, whereupon Gatsby sat down and shaded his eyes and began to laugh.

"It's the funniest thing, old sport," he said hilariously. "I can't—When I try to—"

He had passed visibly through two states and was entering upon a third. After his embarrassment and his unreasoning joy he was consumed with wonder at her presence. He had been full of the idea so long, dreamed it right through to the end, waited with his teeth set, so to speak, at an inconceivable pitch of intensity. Now, in the reaction, he was running down like an overwound clock.

Recovering himself in a minute he opened for us two hulking patent cabinets which held his massed suits and dressing-gowns and ties, and his shirts, piled like bricks in stacks a dozen high.

"I've got a man in England who buys me clothes. He sends over a selection of things at the beginning of each season, spring and fall."

He took out a pile of shirts and began throwing them, one by one, before us, shirts of sheer linen and thick silk and fine flannel, which lost their folds as they fell and covered the table in many-coloured disarray. While we admired he brought more and the soft rich heap mounted higher—shirts with stripes and scrolls and plaids in coral and apple-green and lavender and faint orange, with monograms of Indian blue. Suddenly, with a strained sound, Daisy bent her head into the shirts and began to cry stormily.

"They're such beautiful shirts," she sobbed, her voice muffled in the thick folds. "It makes me sad because I've never seen such—such beautiful shirts before."[5]

If I were a critic, I could tell you what the shirts symbolized and probably someone has already. Personally, I don't think that they were meant to symbolize anything. We are shown them, and because we are shown them properly, we are also shown what Gatsby feels about Daisy and what Daisy feels about Gatsby. And, without being told in as many words, we know that she doesn't return his love. The visit to his house is a diversion, something to kill time; his adoration is mildly flattering, a little pathetic: The end of their story is here foreshadowed. It's all there in the pile of shirts.

Now let us, to make it more difficult, examine a passage from Anthony Powell's *The Acceptance World*, describing the interior of the Ufford, the favourite hotel of his Uncle Giles.

On most of the occasions when I visited the Ufford, halls and reception rooms were so utterly deserted that the interior might almost have been Uncle Giles's private residence. Had he been a rich bachelor, instead of a poor one, he would probably have lived in a house of just that sort: bare: anonymous: old-fashioned: draughty: with heavy mahogany cabinets and sideboards spaced out at intervals in passages and on landings; nothing that could possibly commit him to any specific opinion, beyond general disapproval of the way the world was run.

We always had tea in an apartment called "the lounge", the back half of a large double drawing-room, the inner doors of which were kept permanently closed, thus detaching "the lounge" from "the writing-room", the half overlooking the street. (Perhaps, like the doors of the Temple of Janus, they were closed only in time of Peace; because, years later, when I saw the Ufford in wartime these particular doors had been thrown wide open.) The lace-curtained windows of the lounge gave on to a well; a bleak outlook, casting the gloom of perpetual night, or of a sky for ever dark with rain. Even in summer the electric light had to be switched on during tea.

The wallpaper's intricate floral design in blue, grey, and green ran upwards from a cream-coloured lincrusta dado to a cornice also of cream lincrusta. The pattern of flowers, infinitely faded, closely matched the chintz-covered sofa and armchairs, which were roomy and unexpectedly comfortable. A palm in a brass pot with ornamental handles stood in one corner: here and there were small tables of Moorish design upon each of which had been placed a heavy white globular ash-tray, equipped with an attachment upon which to rest a cigar or cigarette. Several circular gilt looking-glasses hung about the walls, but there was only one picture, an engraving placed over the fireplace, of Landseer's *Bolton Abbey in the Olden Time.* Beneath this crowded scene of medieval plenty—presenting a painful contrast with the Ufford's *cuisine*—a clock, so constructed that pendulum and internal works were visible under its glass dome, stood eternally at twenty minutes past five. Two radiators kept the room reasonably warm in winter, and the coal, surrounded in the fireplace with crinkled pink paper, was never alight. No sign of active life was apparent in the room except for several much-thumbed copies of the *Lady* lying in a heap on one of the Moorish tables.[6]

The Ufford is described in such detail because it's the nearest thing to a permanent home which Uncle Giles possesses. In describing it Powell also describes Uncle Giles.

There is an enduring bond between Uncle Giles and the hotel: They are both old, shabby, out of the main stream. They survive and in their own way are contented. Hotel and man have come to some sort of arrangement with life—that they will not change, that they will not allow themselves to be disturbed.

If we know what sort of dwelling place suits Uncle Giles, we know about Uncle Giles. We are told about him more directly at the conclusion of the description, and then move into an account of the narrator taking tea with him and the arrival of the mysterious Mrs. Erdleigh.

The novel could have begun with this description of Uncle Giles, and then gone on to the description of the Ufford and the narrator's tea with him. This is the obvious way, and the result would have been to turn the Ufford into a stage set—a sound and solid and workmanlike stage set, but not a real place. And to begin with a general account of Uncle Giles' way of living would mean that we were presented not with a human being, but with the narrator making observations about a human being. It could have worked, since eventually we're going to see Uncle Giles in action, as it were; but it wouldn't have worked half so well.

People are places and places are people. This isn't intended to dazzle you with its originality; it's simply another working rule. Whenever you write about places you also write about people. It isn't always that you mention the people when you write about the place. Sometimes it's necessary, sometimes it isn't. On the whole the best way is to concentrate on making the reader see the place.

The most revealing place of all is the home. Imagine yourself suddenly in the home of a complete stranger. Within five minutes you'll have an accurate general picture of what sort of person he is. There are obvious guides like the kind of books or, for that matter, the absence of books, and the pictures and ornaments and the quality of the furniture. There are different kinds of tidiness from the house-proud to the clinically obsessive; different kinds of untidiness from profusion to squalor. There is over and above it all the atmosphere of a home. Some people have the gift of creating comfort, some have not. But be careful about this. If you describe a home properly, if you see it accurately, there's no need to say anything about the atmosphere. Your description says it for you. Or, to be more precise, your reader instantly makes the inference, just as his eye in the cinema will make the inference of falling between a shot of a man swaying on a windowsill ten stories up and the same man hitting the ground.

This isn't to say that we are exclusively the creatures of our economic environment. We aren't, for instance, made what we are by our homes (using the word in its narrowest sense). We make our homes. We were there first, so to speak. We even make impersonal places like offices and factories bear the imprint of our personality—pin-ups on the wall behind the workbench, trendy executive toys, gold pens, silver mounted portraits on the executive's desk (or, equally revealing, nothing at all).

I ask myself of each description of an interior if it has the Asmodeus touch. Asmodeus was the giant who lifted the roofs from houses to look inside. If a novel is to keep up the reader's excitement all the way through, then the secrets revealed must not only be about the characters. Where there are secrets there are mysteries: Mystery, if we're honest, is a condition of human life. I don't believe that you can be a novelist unless you have this sense of mystery, but novels don't attempt to solve it. They set down what the novelist sees. Never put down your thoughts about life and death and time in the novel.

A problem which you're bound to encounter is the treatment of minor characters. Pay too much attention to them and you confuse the reader. Treat them as extras, anonymous waiters and taxi drivers and shop assistants, and the novel becomes dead whilst they're there. For in real life they are actual beings; if you have dealings with them, you register their appearance and voice. The character concerned sees and hears them; so must the reader. In the first instance you must keep track of what is actually happening, of what is ordered from the waiter, the destination of the taxi, what is purchased from the shop. Once the reader is confused, then all that comes through is dead words, a strong impression that you don't know what is happening either.

Let us examine the beginning of Graham Greene's *A Burnt-Out Case.*

> The cabin-passenger wrote in his diary a parody of Descartes: "I feel discomfort, therefore I am alive," then sat pen in hand with no more to record. The captain in a white soutane stood by the open windows of the saloon reading his breviary. There was not enough air to stir the fringes of his beard. The two of them had been alone together on the river for ten days—alone, that is to say, except for the six members of the African crew and the dozen or so deck-passengers who changed, almost indistinguishably, at each village where they stopped. The boat, which was the property of the Bishop, resembled a small battered Mississippi paddle-steamer with a high nineteenth-century forestructure, the white paint badly in need of renewal. From the saloon windows they could see the river before them unwind, and below them on the pontoons the passengers sat and dressed their hair among the logs of wood for the engine.
>
> If no change means peace, this certainly was peace, to be found like a nut at the centre of the hard shell of discomfort—the heat that engulfed them where the river narrowed to a mere hundred metres: the shower that was

always hot from the ship's engine: in the evening the mosquitoes, and in the day the tsetse flies with wings raked back like tiny jet-fighters (a board above the bank at the last village had warned them in three languages: "Zone of sleeping sickness. Be careful of the tsetse flies"). The captain read his breviary with a fly-whisk in his hand, and whenever he made a kill he held up the tiny corpse for the passenger's inspection, saying "tsetse"—it was nearly the limit of their communication, for neither spoke the other's language with ease or accuracy.[7]

The author is concentrating upon establishing the background; he tells us very little about the cabin-passenger. The description continues: We see "the thick, rapid, khaki-coloured stream"; we hear the sanctus bell calling the people to mass at four in the morning. And we see the cabin-passenger's quarters, "which he shared with a crucifix, a chair, a table, a cupboard where cockroaches lurked, and one picture—the nostalgic photograph of some church in Europe covered in a soutane of heavy snow. . . ."

The author is explicit about it: "This was somewhat the way in which the days passed." And yet, as with the example from Anthony Powell, he's not giving us merely a set piece. The novel isn't about a journey up the Congo; it's about the cabin-passenger.

There yet remained another hour or two of peace towards the end of the day, when he sat below on a pontoon while the Africans prepared their chop in the early dark. The vampire bats creaked over the forest and candles flickered, reminding him of the Benedictions of his youth. The laughter of the cooks went back and forth from one pontoon to the other, and it was never long before someone sang, but he couldn't understand the words.[8]

After dinner the cabin-passenger and the captain talk.

"What are they singing, father?" the cabin-passenger asks about the cooks. "What kind of song? A love song?"

"No," the captain said, "not a love song. They sing only about what has happened during the day, how at the last village they bought some fine cooking-pots which they will sell for a good profit farther up the river, and of course they sing of you and me."

"What do they sing about me?"

"They are singing now, I think." He put the dice and counters away and listened. "Shall I translate for you? It is not altogether complimentary."

"Yes, if you please."

"'Here is a white man who is neither a father nor a doctor. He has no beard. He comes from a long way away—we do not know from where—and he tells no one to what place he is going nor why. He is a rich man, for he drinks whisky every evening and he smokes all the time. Yet he offers no man a cigarette.'"⁹

We haven't seen the singers; though if the cabin-passenger does see them, his reaction will be that they all look alike. In any case, if only because of the language barrier and the circumstances, he has no reason to differentiate between them. They're important because of their singing. They're part of the exotic background. And then comes the shock: They are observing the cabin-passenger; they're describing his character. And so we learn about him not from the author sticking a label on him in the first place, but from the reaction of the natives. This is description in action.

So we will here establish another working rule: Don't describe your characters all in one breath. It's true that in real life we may often notice exceptional physical beauty or ugliness immediately; but even then, there are other features which we don't assimilate immediately. It is action which shows us character: The story is advanced as we advance into the characters.

Mr. Greene's device isn't copyrighted, though of course his words are. Technique is learned only by the study of accomplished technicians and by the adaptation of their technique to your own material. Until the late L. A. G. Strong pointed out this passage in a talk, I hadn't noticed it. In a way you aren't meant to. The device has a very specific function and it performs it. But if you are to write a publishable novel, you must always be on the alert for such passages.

What is never acceptable is the sheer piling up of detail, whether about people or about things. Each aspect of a person must be another surprise, must take us further into the story; the same applies to things, particularly man-made things. I emphasize this because of the nature of the world in which I—and most of my readers—live. This is a world in which even the earth under our feet is to a large extent shaped by man. The objects which influence our daily lives are shaped or influenced by man. For the most part we don't wrest our living direct from the earth. We live in a world of man-made objects, some of which we choose for ourselves. The majority of us have strong feelings about all of these objects, whether or not we are articulate about them. They wouldn't exist if we didn't need them.

To be a novelist you must understand what the majority of people feel about the material world. Whether it's right or wrong to live so much in a world shaped by man is beside the point. Whether it's right or wrong for the majority of people to attach so much importance to material things is beside the point. (I have noticed myself that those who are loudest in their denunciation of materialism are precisely those who have taken good care to secure for themselves an abundance of material things.) It isn't your job as a novelist to try to change this state of affairs. You don't have the time.

And here, out of order, I put down another rule: Time spent in thinking about anything else but one's craft and the material of that craft, which is the whole visible, tangible world, is wasted time. And there's another rule rising out of this: The only acceptable system of government for the writer is one which allows people to drop out, to huddle together in dusty, seedy, cosy corners and make a mess of their lives in their own way. I say this, and pass on. You understand it or you don't, and if you don't, you may as well stop reading the book here and now.

What you must now consider—and having considered it, put it in the back of your mind—is that you're writing for the future. What the sword, the spear, the cloak, the war-horse, the castle, are to us now, so it will be with the Beretta, the Burberry, the Mini, the Georgian style detached. This doesn't mean that you're to see any object as a symbol. You have only to realize that both sword and pistol, for example, are weapons. To describe them accurately—which includes describing accurately what they're like in action and what their effects are—is what counts. This is difficult, but it is even more difficult when it comes to the Burberry.

I choose this example as denoting a particular quality of raincoat. It illustrates the evocative property of a brand name. If one of your characters owns a Burberry, it instantly imparts information about him. He isn't poor, he may even be rich. He may either simply want a solid and durable article, or he may have a picture of himself as a country gentleman, as in the brand image. But, there being so many makes of raincoat available in a consumer society, his choice of that particular make must prove something about him.

There are times when to use brand names is not only unrealistic but faintly ludicrous. There are times when the brand name is enough to describe something, and times when there must be some amplification (though you mustn't forget that the laws of libel apply in this field too).

Again, you must play it by ear. If it sounds right, it is right. There are no reference books to help you. And if there were, they'd have to be continually revised. Brands appear and disappear, are fashionable and unfashionable, and there is a continual process of change. The choice of a Pierce-Arrow is exactly right in the O'Hara novel, the period being the twenties; if you have one of your characters buy a new Pierce-Arrow now, then the whole novel will be flawed, since they went out of manufacture in 1938. I don't suppose that anyone would be likely to make this particular sort of mistake, but equally glaring mistakes are made.

To be accurate about the physical world is difficult. To come back to the beginning, it forces us to see (and hear and feel and smell) what we're writing about. Because it's difficult, the majority of British novelists—far more than the majority of Americans—dodge it as much as they can. (As for the use of brand names, I honestly believe that they consider it vulgar.)

This is hard luck on the reader, but it's your good luck. Though in the strictest sense novel writing isn't competitive, you still must remember those thousands of other novels which aren't as readable as they could be. If their authors choose to run hobbled at the ankles, then you're bound to get ahead of them. (To be frank, whenever I feel depressed about my own novels—which is often—I look at other people's; the sparseness of their texture, their total lack of vitality, always cheer me up.) Of course, there are other ways of writing a readable novel than mine. But mine is acceptable both to British and American readers. I don't promise you instant success, but neither do I offer theories which are unproved in practice.

FOUR: A good beginning means a good book

My first axiom as a reviewer was that a good beginning means a good book. A good beginning is one which takes the reader straight into the action. It must also tell us who and what the novel will be about. It doesn't give away the story, but it doesn't leave us in any doubt. It shouldn't ever begin with a foreword, nor should it be leisurely and discursive. Summary—"This is the story of what happened to an ordinary English family in the year of the Apollo moonshot" —must never be used. It need not mention the main characters, but it's much preferable that they be brought in straight away.

Because my first draft of my first novel is the only first draft available to me, I shall use it as an example. Originally I began with Joe Lampton visiting Warley, the small Yorkshire town where the main action of the novel is to take place, on a bicycle trip at the age of seventeen. I intended to contrast Warley with Dufton, the drab little industrial town where he then lives. Warley was to stay in his mind as his dream town; his love for it was to grow during the war years. He was then to get a job there, actually to live there; what I had in mind was to make absolutely explicit what he felt about Warley— for what people feel about places can be as important as what they feel about human beings.

But this raised a problem, which was how to deal with the war years. I didn't think it satisfactory to summarize them; but to cut from 1939 to 1946 would break the flow of the narrative, leave the reader wondering exactly when it was all happening. It was indeed necessary to show what kind of home Joe had and how different Dufton was from Warley; but there had to be some better way of doing it. The novel wasn't to be about his life in Dufton, but about what happened to him when he came to Warley. So the bicycle trip to Warley wasn't narrative but preamble. I wasn't going immediately into the action, I was setting the stage. In fact, the whole chapter was the equivalent of the leisurely chat by the old butler in Act One about the changes at the Hall since the new Master came into his inheritance.

Then I decided that the third-person narration was wrong for this novel. It was forcing me into a God's-eye point of view which didn't suit me, which I wasn't mature enough to handle. I wanted to give the reader the impression of a man talking directly to him, talking at his ease, holding nothing back. And I wanted my style to be colloquial, to give me elbowroom to comment and summarize. It was, of course, a question of finding the right tone of voice: I think that from the moment I took the decision to go straight into the story, this came with it.

This is only one way, the way which suited me. It's the easiest and most obvious, and the most reliable. It doesn't matter that it's so often used; the way in which you use it is what will make your novel original. There is no copyright in literary devices, only in words.

Indeed, it is absolutely essential that you look at novelists you admire and see how they do it. I'll take for my first example the opening of Anthony Powell's *A Question of Upbringing*, which is the first novel in his *A Dance to the Music of Time* sequence:

The men at work at the corner of the street had made a kind of camp for themselves, where, marked out by tripods hung with red hurricane-lamps, an abyss in the road led down to a network of subterranean drain-pipes. Gathered round the bucket of coke that burned in front of the shelter, several figures were swinging arms against bodies and rubbing hands together with large, pantomimic gestures: like comedians giving formal expression to the concept of extreme cold. One of them, a spare fellow in blue overalls, taller than the rest, with a jocular demeanour and long, pointed nose like that of a Shakespearian clown, suddenly stepped forward, and, as if performing a rite, cast some substance—apparently the remains of two kippers, loosely wrapped in newspaper—on the bright coals of the fire, causing flames to leap fiercely upwards, smoke curling about in eddies of the north-east wind. As the dark fumes floated above the houses, snow began to fall gently from a dull sky, each flake giving a small hiss as it reached the bucket. The flames died down again. And the men, as if required observances were for the moment at an end, all turned away from the fire, lowering themselves laboriously into the pit, or withdrawing to the shadows of their tarpaulin shelter. The grey, undecided flakes continued to come down, though not heavily, while a harsh odour, bitter and gaseous, penetrated the air. The day was drawing in.

For some reason, the sight of snow descending on fire always makes me think of the ancient world—legionaries in sheepskin warming themselves at a brazier: mountain altars where offerings glow between wintry pillars; centaurs with torches cantering beside a frozen sea—scattered, uncoordinated shapes from a fabulous past, infinitely removed from life; and yet bringing with them memories of things real and imagined. These classical projections, and something in the physical attitudes of the men themselves as they turned from the fire, suddenly suggested Poussin's scene in which the Seasons, hand in hand and facing outward, tread in rhythm to the notes of the lyre that the winged and naked greybeard plays. The image of Time brought thoughts of mortality: of human beings, facing outward like the Seasons, moving hand in hand in intricate measure: stepping slowly, methodically, sometimes a trifle awkwardly, in evolutions that take recognizable shape: or breaking into seemingly meaningless gyrations, while partners disappear only to reappear again, once more giving pattern to the spectacle: unable to control the melody, unable, perhaps, to control the steps of the dance. Classical associations made me think, too, of days at school, where so many forces, hitherto unfamiliar, had become in due course uncompromisingly clear.[10]

There is a break of a line—take note of this as an example of the proper use of spacing—and we move to the description of the narrator's school and the road which runs westward of it. Then Widmerpool appears:

By this stage of the year—exercise no longer contestable five days a week—the road was empty; except for Widmerpool, in a sweater once white and cap at least a size too small, hobbling unevenly, though with determination, on the flat heels of spiked running-shoes. Slowly but surely he loomed through the dusk towards me as I walked back—well wrapped-up, I remember—from an expedition to the High Street. Widmerpool was known to go voluntarily for "a run" by himself every afternoon. This was his return from trotting across the plough in drizzle that had been falling since early school. I had, of course, often seen him before, because we were in the same house; even spoken with him, though he was a bit older than myself. Anecdotes relating to his acknowledged oddness were also familiar; but before that moment such stories had not made him live. It was on the bleak December tarmac of that Saturday afternoon in, I suppose, the year 1921 that Widmerpool, fairly heavily built, thick lips and metal-

John Braine

rimmed spectacles giving his face as usual an aggrieved expression, first took coherent form in my mind. As the damp, insistent cold struck up from the road, two thin jets of steam drifted out of his nostrils, by nature much distended, and all at once he seemed to possess a painful solidarity that talk about him had never conveyed. Something comfortless and inelegant in his appearance suddenly impressed itself on the observer, as stiffly, almost majestically, Widmerpool moved on his heels out of the mist.[11]

The sequence isn't about Widmerpool. He isn't in the usual sense of the word its hero. (Neither is Nick Jenkins, the narrator.) But he is the central figure, he dominates the sequence. When he enters, the narrative begins. What the sequence is about we have been told—not the passing of time, but the music of time, the ordered pattern of time. It is explicitly a story of time remembered; the narrator's position is firmly in the present, looking back. We are led from the description of the workmen on a winter's day to the description of Poussin's picture and so back to the narrator's schooldays. The transition is absolutely natural and unforced because the description of the winter's day is absolutely concrete. We are there, we hear the hiss of the snow falling on the coke, smell its bitter and gaseous odour. Most important, the novel doesn't begin with abstractions; it takes us into an absolutely authentic reality—a reality, what is more, which is on the face of it commonplace.

John O'Hara's *Appointment in Samarra* is the story of one man, Julian English, the president of the Gibbsville-Cadillac Motor Car Company. Julian has it made, is secure in his place in Gibbsville society, and then on a drunken impulse, throws his drink in the face of Harry Reilly, an Irish bootlegger, at the Gibbsville Country Club. From then on Gibbsville turns against him and he is hounded to his death. Most writers would have begun with the key event in the country club, or at least begun with Julian.

O'Hara—and this was his first novel—began with Luther Fliegler and his wife:

> Our story opens in the mind of Luther L. (L. for LeRoy) Fliegler, who is lying in his bed, not thinking of anything, but just aware of sounds, conscious of his own breathing, and sensitive to his own heartbeats. Lying beside him is his wife, lying on her right side and enjoying her sleep. She has earned her sleep, for it is Christmas morning, strictly speaking, and all the day before she has worked like a dog, cleaning the turkey and baking things, and, until a few hours ago, trimming the tree. The awful proximity of his heartbeats make Luther Fliegler begin to want his wife a little, but Irma can say no when she is tired. It is too much trouble, she says when she is tired, and she won't take any chances. Three children is enough; three children in ten years. So Luther Fliegler does not reach out for her. It is Christmas morning, and he will do her the favour of letting her enjoy her sleep: a favour which she will never know he did for her. And it is a favour, all right, because Irma likes Christmas too, and on this one morning she might not mind the trouble, might be willing to take a chance. Luther Fliegler more actively stifled the little temptation and thought the hell with it, and then turned and put his hands around his wife's waist and caressed the little rubber tire of flesh across her diaphragm. She began to stir and then she opened her eyes and said: "My God, Lute, what are you doing?"
>
> "Merry Christmas," he said.
>
> "Don't, will you please?" she said, but she smiled happily and put her arms around his big back. "God, you're crazy," she said. "Oh, but I love you." And for a little while Gibbsville knew no happier people than Luther

71

Fliegler and his wife, Irma. Then Luther went to sleep, and Irma got up and then came back to the bedroom, stopping to look out the window before she got into bed again.

Lantenengo Street had a sort of cottony silence to it. The snow was piled high in the gutters, and the street was open only to the width of two cars. It was too dark for the street to look cottony, and there was an illusion even about the silence. Irma thought she could yell her loudest and not be heard, so puffily silent did it look, but she also knew that if she wanted to (which she didn't) she could carry on a conversation with Mrs. Bromberg across the way, without either of them raising her voice. Irma chided herself for thinking this way about Mrs. Bromberg on Christmas morning, but immediately she defended herself: Jews do not observe Christmas, except to make more money out of Christmas, so you do not have to treat Jews any different on Christmas than on any other day of the year. Besides, having the Brombergs on Lantenengo Street hurt real-estate values. Everybody said so. The Brombergs, Lute had it on good authority, had paid thirty thousand for the Price property, which was twelve thousand five hundred more than Will Price had been asking; but if the Brombergs wanted to live on Lantenengo Street, they could pay for it. Irma wondered if it was true that Sylvia Bromberg's sister and brother-in-law were dickering for the McAdams' property next door. She wouldn't be surprised. Pretty soon there would be a whole colony of Jews in the neighbourhood, and the Fliegler children and all the other nice children in the neighbourhood would grow up with Jewish accents.[12]

On the face of it, Luther has nothing to do with Julian. It transpires, however, that he's one of Julian's salesmen. They aren't rich, but they get along. "Lute was right: he figured that if you sell two Cadillacs a month, you make expenses, and anything over that is so much gravy. . . ." And next year they'll do better, and Irma and Luther will join the country club—"and it would be a good thing, because Lute would be able to make better contacts and sell more Cadillacs to club members. . . ." But they won't join until they can afford it. Then comes the transition. "Twenty after three," Irma thinks. "The country club dance would just be getting good. . . ." She thinks with love of Lute, "dependable and honest as the day is long, and never looked at another woman, even in fun. . . ." The transition is made with wonderful smoothness: we're listening to Irma, who isn't interested in Julian, only in Lute. "If she had married, say, Julian English, she could be a member of the club, but she wouldn't trade her life for Caroline English's, not if you paid her. She wondered if Julian and Caroline were having another of their battle royals. . . ."[13]

But the next episode isn't about one of Julian and Caroline's battle royals. We're given a picture of the people present at the country club dance, then concentrate on Julian, who's looking at Harry Reilly with increasing dislike—a dislike which is based on nothing more substantial than Reilly's being a vulgarian and a social climber. He knows also that it would be most unwise to offend him, since he virtually owns the Gibbsville-Cadillac Motor Car Company. The actual throwing of the drink is not described directly, or indeed in any detail.

> The stag line was scattered all over the floor by the time the band was working on the second chorus of the tune, and when Johnny Dibble suddenly appeared, breathless, at the place where his cronies customarily stood, there were only two young men for him to address. "Jeez," he said. "Jeezozz H. Kee-rist. You hear about what just happened?"
>
> "No. No," they said.
>
> "You didn't? About Julian English?"
>
> "No. No. What was it?"

73

"Julian English. He just threw a highball in Harry Reilly's face. Jeest!"[14]

We are in a different world from that of Luther and Irma Fliegler, which is wholesome, orderly, and based on love. To show us this world in the beginning makes us see all the more vividly the near-saturnalia of the country club. The violence of Julian's literally suicidal action is all the more shocking: We move from the act of love to the act of hate. But if this were all, the beginning would be too clever by half. O'Hara means it when he says that the story begins in the mind of Luther L. Fliegler. For Luther's job depends upon Julian's not being so foolish as to throw his drink into the face of a rich and influential man. Julian's action is going to affect Luther most directly. Willy-nilly, Luther will be damaged too, his contentment with his life taken away, his plans for the future brought to nothing.

There is something even more important to be noted about the first chapter which, incidentally, runs only to four pages. We have been told when and where and what and whom. O'Hara hasn't concerned himself with giving us a detailed description of a small town in Pennsylvania during Prohibition. He has shown us a car salesman in bed with his wife in the small hours of Christmas morning. He and his wife say and think nothing which would not be completely natural to them.

The fascination is in the details. A lesser writer would have had Irma think in a generalized sort of way about Prohibition, the false values of the rich, the desirability of Lantenengo Street as a residential area and so on. Certainly there would have been a great deal more about Julian and Julian's way of life. But we begin with her dislike of her Jewish neighbour, Mrs. Bromberg, and her satisfaction at the inflated price the Brombergs have had to pay for their house. A lesser writer, again, couldn't have resisted the opportunity to make some judgement on anti-Semitism. But O'Hara knew that to make judgements isn't the business of the novelist.

All the information about Julian's world is given in passing. We learn the necessary facts about Luther and Irma. This isn't to say that it would have been wrong to have started at the country club. In fact, it would be a useful exercise for you to visualize the novel with the first chapter eliminated.

It is interesting to note that O'Hara wrote very quickly and revised little. I doubt if he planned very much. This is not to say that he wasn't an accomplished craftsman, with a live sense of form; there is nothing loose or rambling about the novel. I believe that it is this which gives this novel and his work in general its compulsive narrative flow and relentless pace. But, although I don't believe that he planned in any detail, my instincts tell me that he knew how the novel would end when he began it.

What I am saying boils down to this: Direct statement isn't the only possible method. The apparently circuitous route can be the quickest. What at all costs you must do is to keep yourself out of it—to keep yourself out of it even when you're writing in the first person.

In my own instance the first chapter of *Room at the Top* isn't directly about the hero Joe Lampton. It's about Joe's reactions to Warley. Of course it reveals Joe's character; but what I was primarily concerned with was making the reader see Warley. If I got Warley right, I'd get Joe right. I would be also going straight into the story. The love affair is not only between Joe and Alice, but between Joe and Warley. What happens between Joe and the town is a *coup de foudre*, a thunderstroke of mutual attraction.

But let us now consider a beginning which is in every sense of the word direct, that of Alan Sillitoe's *Saturday Night and Sunday Morning*.

John Braine

The rowdy gang of singers who sat at the scattered tables saw Arthur walk unsteadily to the head of the stairs, and though they must all have known that he was dead drunk, and seen the danger he would soon be in, no one attempted to talk to him and lead him back to his seat. With eleven pints of beer and seven small gins playing hide-and-seek inside his stomach, he fell from the topmost stair to the bottom.

It was Benefit Night for the White Horse Club, and the pub had burst its contribution box and spread a riot through its rooms and between its four walls. Floors shook and windows rattled, and leaves of aspidistras wilted in the fumes of beer and smoke. Notts County had beaten the visiting team, and the members of the White Horse supporters club were quartered upstairs to receive a flow of victory. Arthur was not a member of the club, but Brenda was, and so he was drinking the share of her absent husband—as far as it would go—and when the club went bust and the shrewd publican put on the towels for those that couldn't pay, he laid eight half-crowns on the table, intending to fork out for his own.

For it was Saturday night, the best and bingiest glad-time of the week, one of the fifty-two holidays in the slow-turning Big Wheel of the year, a violent preamble to a prostrate Sabbath. Piled-up passions were exploded on Saturday night, and the effect of a week's monotonous graft in the factory was swilled out of your system in a burst of goodwill. You followed the motto of "be drunk and be happy", kept your crafty arms around female waists, and felt the beer going beneficially down into the elastic capacity of your guts. [15]

There is no building-up of tension, only the briefest description of the background, and no description of the character. There is one exact detail, the eleven pints of beer

76

and seven small gins, which is enough to make the fall credible and to give us a secondary shock.

What follows is the drinking match which led him to swallow eleven pints of beer and seven small gins; we then fall with him down the steps again:

> He was laughing to himself as he rolled down the stairs, at the dull bumping going on behind his head and along his spine, as if it were happening miles away, like a vibration on another part of the earth's surface, and he an earthquake-machine on which it was faintly recorded. This rolling motion was so restful and soporific, in fact, that when he stopped travelling—having arrived at the bottom of the stairs—he kept his eyes closed and went to sleep. It was a pleasant and faraway feeling, and he wanted to stay in exactly the same position for the rest of his life.[16]

The first paragraph has the effect of someone rushing in excitedly—the author is bringing us a headline from Arthur Seaton's world. We read on because we want to know what happened to Arthur; but if at this point we were told, the story would slacken, we might even put the book aside. Instead we are told about the drinking match and, incidentally, something more about Arthur and the way he spends his Saturday nights; after the description of his sensations during the fall itself comes the description of his feelings as he lies on the floor. He feels strangely comfortable and happy, his chief desire being to go to sleep. He is pulled to his feet by a waiter and suddenly comes to his senses, apparently quite sober. The story is back in the present; but the flashback has had another function. It has conveyed to us the sense of the tricks that alcohol plays with time; in Arthur's mind what actually happened before his fall might equally as well have happened after.

It should also be noted that the author never explicitly states that Arthur is uninjured. Nor does he ask himself whether he's injured or not. This is partly because he's drunk, and if anything has rather enjoyed the fall, and partly because he isn't the sort of person to worry about it; he takes life as it comes. Again, information is given incidentally, not directly, revealed through action, not hung round the character's neck like a placard.

It isn't my intention, however, to compile an annotated anthology of beginnings. I do suggest that you compile your own, that you analyze the beginning of any novel that you have read with pleasure in order that you may discover how the author achieves his effects. Your aim must always be to write in a way which is entirely your own, but literary devices are common property.

I must add that the literary merit of the novels which you examine isn't of the least consequence. It's enough that their beginning made you read on. Neither is their genre of the least consequence. What is an excellent way to begin a thriller may well be an excellent way to begin a straight novel.

I do not recommend that you study the novels now accepted as classics. I take it for granted that you'll have read them and will reread them with increasing profit to yourself; as we grow older, the great writers give us more and more. But too many commentators have been there before you—and mostly academics at that. And what worked for them won't necessarily work for you. In fact, it almost certainly won't. A great writer is a great writer for all time, but he is also absolutely of his own time.

So you mustn't limit yourself in any way. Take whatever you need from wherever you need it. It should go without saying that you don't copy any other writer's style or characters or background or plot—using the word copy, of course, in its strictest sense.

The paradox is that the beginning used by another writer, if it instinctively seems right for you, becomes entirely original when you use it. In any case, it's more than likely that the other writer took it from someone else in the first place. What is taken is a container, not what is in the container. The container is common property. What is in it is yours and yours alone.

To write about beginnings is to write about chapter beginnings. It's incredible when I look back, but until I actually began the final draft of my first novel I hadn't given any thought to the business of beginning a chapter. What I did realize was that to begin each in the same way would produce a monotonous effect. So, as I recommend now to others, I did myself; I simply took, as it were, from the common store. It wasn't quite as easy as it appeared, for the beginning determined the tone of the whole chapter. It had to be as arresting as the beginning of the book, it had to contain action, the dancing ball that was the story never had to dance in exactly the direction the reader anticipated.

A word here about titles and epigraphs. I needn't stress the importance of a good title. There aren't any formulas for devising one, only general principles. The first is that it should tell you what the novel is about. That it should be striking, original, easy to remember and to pronounce, is also important; but you're far more likely to achieve all this if you first of all concentrate upon the job of expressing what the novel is about in the minimum number of words.

It's better not to be too clever, and if you use a quotation, it shouldn't be a hackneyed one. (If I were a publisher's reader, I should automatically reject any novel with a title taken from *Hamlet* or *Macbeth*.) Failing all else, it's worth considering a quotation from one of your own characters. For in hunting for a suitable one, you're almost forced to discover the theme.

The epigraph is optional. It should make a comment upon the theme rather than summarize it. And the full force of the

comment shouldn't be understood until after the book has
been read. You shouldn't have to hunt for an epigraph. It can
be anything you like from a joke to an advertisement, but it
should stick in your mind in connection with the novel.

A good title won't in itself sell a novel, or a bad title hinder
it. You can do worse than simply use the main character's
name or the name of the most important place in the novel.
But it makes sense to do anything that you can to set your
novel apart from all the thousands of other novels.

FIVE: Dialogue

Dialogue must always be speakable. I apologize for being so obvious, but if this book doesn't dare to be obvious, it will be useless. The working rule is this: If you can't speak it aloud, it's no good. Unless you're willing to expend the time to apply this test, you shouldn't attempt to write a novel. It goes without saying that you should do no more than indicate the repetitiousness and incoherences and unfinished sentences of actual speech.

You must of course learn how to listen. As far as is consistent with your temperament, apply the techniques of the professional interviewer in daily life. What this boils down to is learning to ask questions which cannot be answered by a simple yes or no, and learning how to convey the impression of all-consuming interest in the speaker. It's also necessary to learn how to merge into the background, how sometimes to appear as if you're not listening at all.

If you don't do this, then there's no way of learning how to write good dialogue. All books on idiom are out of date as soon as they're written. This is inescapable. Usage and idiom change all the time. But this is only the general pattern. Everyone doesn't change simultaneously. And there are some people who are always out-of-date in their idiom or who use it incorrectly. A novel in which all the characters used idiom which was exactly right for the period would be absolutely unreal.

To complicate matters still further, it's not always

necessary that your idiom and usage be correct. You can write superb dialogue which will have very little relation to the way in which people actually speak. (The rule about it being speakable still holds good.) It might well be that this is how you hear people, what you translate unconsciously into an English of your own. If it sounds right to the reader, then it is right. The writing of a novel is an art, not a science, and the novel is an infinitely flexible medium. A novel is a work of fiction, not a sociological report. Listen, but not too much; in the end it's the voices inside your head which are the most authentic.

But don't carry this business of writing for the ear too far. When a speaker has a regional or foreign accent, or uses broad dialect, or has some marked peculiarity of pronunciation, it is fatal to attempt to produce it phonetically. Another rule comes into force here: If it doesn't look right, if it is more difficult to read than it would be to listen to in real life, then put it in Standard English. The English alphabet isn't suited for phonetics. It is enough to indicate, outside the dialogue, the special way of speaking; what most accurately conveys the essence of a region, for instance, are the expressions and constructions which are peculiar to the region.

Generally speaking, if you wish to convey that someone has, for instance, a broad Northumbrian accent, then simply say so. If it's very broad, then you can make a brief approximation of what it sounds like phonetically, then say that whoever is listening translates it into plain English, and continue in plain English. In point of fact, this is the most realistic way of doing it; faced with an unfamiliar accent, we're slightly puzzled at first, then rapidly become used to it. And even when faced with unfamiliar expressions or familiar expressions used in an unfamiliar way, we understand by the context. In fact, regardless of how the words are delivered, we manage to get their message—or as much of it as we want to get.

As an example of how it ought to be done, here is a passage from James Joyce's *Ulysses*:

—The blessings of God on you, Buck Mulligan cried, jumping from his chair. Sit down. Pour out the tea there. The sugar is in the bag. Here, I can't go fumbling at the damned eggs. He hacked through the fry on the dish and slapped it out on three plates, saying:
—*In nomine Patris et Filii et Spiritus Sancti.*
Haines sat down to pour out the tea.
—I'm giving you two lumps each, he said. But, I say, Mulligan, you do make strong tea, don't you?
Buck Mulligan, hewing thick slices from the loaf, said in an old woman's wheedling voice:
—When I makes tea I makes tea, as old mother Grogan said. And when I makes water I makes water.
—By Jove, it is tea, Haines said.
Buck Mulligan went on hewing and wheedling:
—So I do, Mrs. Cahill, says she. Begob, ma'am, says Mrs. Cahill, God send you don't make them in the one pot. . . .

The doorway was darkened by an entering form.
—The milk, sir.
—Come in, ma'am, Mulligan said. Kinch, get the jug.
An old woman came forward and stood by Stephen's elbow.
—That's a lovely morning, sir, she said. Glory be to God.
—To whom? Mulligan said, glancing at her. Ah, to be sure.
Stephen reached back and took the milkjug from the locker.
—The islanders, Mulligan said to Haines casually, speak frequently of the collector of prepuces.

—How much, sir? asked the old woman.
—A quart, Stephen said. . . .

—It is indeed, ma'am, Buck Mulligan said, pouring milk into their cups.
—Taste it, sir, she said.
He drank at her bidding.
—If we could only live on good food like that, he said to her somewhat loudly, we wouldn't have the country full of rotten teeth and rotten guts. Living in a bogswamp, eating cheap food and the streets paved with dust, horsedung and consumptives' spits.
—Are you a medical student, sir? the old woman asked.
—I am, ma'am, Buck Mulligan answered. . . .

—Do you understand what he says? Stephen asked her.
—Is it French you are talking, sir? the old woman said to Haines.
Haines spoke to her again a longer speech, confidently.
—Irish, Buck Mulligan said. Is there Gaelic on you?
—I thought it was Irish, she said, by the sound of it. Are you from the west, sir?
—I am an Englishman, Haines answered.
—He's English, Buck Mulligan said, and he thinks we ought to speak Irish in Ireland.
—Sure we ought to, the old woman said, and I'm ashamed I don't speak the language myself. I'm told it's a grand language by them that knows.
—Grand is no name for it, said Buck Mulligan. Wonderful entirely. Fill us out some more tea, Kinch. Would you like a cup, ma'am?[17]

There are four different voices here. We're told at the beginning that Haines is English; even if we hadn't been, it would have been obvious from his way of speaking—"I say,

Mulligan, you do make strong tea. . . ." Buck Mulligan and Stephen have the clear enunciation of the educated Dubliner; we can hear Mulligan thicken his accent when he says "in an old woman's wheedling voice" what old mother Grogan says about making tea. The old woman who brings in the milk speaks differently again. She has what neo-Irish call the brogue; this is instantly established without any *shures* or *begorrahs* or *bejabers* or even a dropped consonant.

The question of class is of course inextricably linked—at least in England—with regional accent. It isn't as simple as once it was, however. You can no longer say that only Standard English is socially acceptable (and a slight Irish or Scottish accent). However, you can't say that Standard English is ever a handicap, and there still are professions in which you can't do without it. All other things being equal, of two candidates for a job, one speaking Standard English and the other with a regional accent, the former gets the job. It doesn't matter very much about my own Yorkshire accent, for instance; for radio and television it's a positive advantage. But I should have gone to some pains to get rid of it if I'd been a barrister or stockbroker. (Though in that case I should almost certainly have been public-school educated, so wouldn't have had it.) It isn't possible within the terms of reference of this book to be any more specific than this: Standard English remains the only approved accent of the upper and upper-middle classes, but in what, for want of a better phrase, I'll call King's Road Society, it may be replaced by a variation, which is Cockney-based, essentially self-parodying. The implication of the self-parody is that its user could speak Standard English if he wanted. This accent is rather camp—implying also some sort of connection with show business and excitement in general—and is sometimes called classless. It's easy to assume if you're on the way up, and can be used by those already up so as not to appear snobbish, and also as an act of mild rebellion against their elders and the establishment.

This accent is often combined with a mildly American idiom and a rougher intonation in business and particularly in the mass media. Here the implication is quite deliberately that not class but achievement matters, and that you're only interested in results. At the same time you don't want there to be any barriers between you and whoever is the object of your attention.

None of this is of the least value to you as a writer unless you find it out for yourself. Miss Nancy Mitford's book[18] on U and Non-U still remains valuable, though since its publication I should imagine that the Upper Classes have taken deliberately to using Non-U words like "sweet" for "pudding" and "toilet" for "lavatory." But even if it had been totally inaccurate from the date of its publication, it would be useful, if only to drive the fact home that the Upper Classes still exist in England and that their way of speaking is essentially less constrained than that of other classes, because they believe that whatever they do is right. This should go without saying, but what ruins many novels is the inability of their authors to realize such simple truths.

John O'Hara once remarked that no one who had got beyond high school ever used the term half-a-dollar and that if you had a graduate use the expression, then you'd have made that character totally unreal. And, he said, there was no book that would tell you about such things. If you've got what he called a tin ear, that's it. If you don't observe the world around you, that's it. I remember, for instance, in the film based on my novel *Room at the Top,* that the circle around Joe Lampton's mistress in London was represented as sneering at his Yorkshire accent and background. Since they were all connected with the mass media, the exact opposite would have been the case. To be provincial—particularly

Yorkshire—and working class has been trendy since the late fifties.

Again, I remember some four years ago an eminent author waxing indignant about the contemporary misuse of language. He cited as an example hearing at a party that a girl had gone gay. Very plainly the eminent author understood by this that she had become a prostitute. She meant, of course, that she'd turned lesbian. The word had that meaning then, and had had for some years before. How could he not have known it? And how could he have failed to realize that the sort of girl who would be spoken about at the sort of parties he went to wouldn't announce her taking up prostitution, and if she did, wouldn't announce it in that way? She would actually either say that she'd decided to shack up with a particular man or that she'd decided to live on men.

I remember, too, the late Brendan Behan saying that the trouble with middle-class writers like Braine was that they didn't know how the working classes talked. For instance, a writer like Braine would have characters refer to a tart as meaning a prostitute, but in working-class idiom a tart was simply a girl—you'd say that your fiancée was a nice tart. If Behan had looked at my second novel, *From the Hand of the Hunter*, published some years before, he'd have found the word used in the working-class sense. I was perfectly familiar with it in both the working-class and middle-class sense. But he had a point: If you did have a working-class character call a prostitute a tart, then you'd have him saying something which he wouldn't ever say in real life.

But you don't have to be a philologist, much less a sociologist, in order to write good dialogue. You need only have a good ear. It's possible to know too much, to become more interested in the words themselves than in what they add up to. The basic purpose of dialogue is to show character. There is no law which decrees that dialogue must always

87

reveal region and class. It's perfectly possible to select what your characters say so as to make these considerations irrelevant.

The American novelist is, because of the far greater variety and richness of U.S. idiom and accent, in a far stronger position than the British novelist. It's always seemed to me that it should be virtually impossible for an American novelist to write bad dialogue.

Apart from any other consideration, there isn't in the U.S. an equivalent accent to Standard English. I suppose that the Boston Brahmin accent would come nearest to it; but what would count in speech would be simply to avoid mistakes in grammar and pronunciation. I'll put it this way: On the level of the British High Court judge, the only accent you'll ever hear is Standard English or a faint Scottish or Irish, but at the equivalent level in the U.S. I should expect a wide assortment of regional accents.

What would seem a great waste if I were an American novelist would be to limit the speech of my characters to one kind. It would be inaccurate, because within most American communities there is a wider variety of accents than in Britain. The reason is that Americans move around more. I don't mean that isolated communities with a few immigrants don't exist, or that the novelist may not for his own purposes elect to have his characters use the same accent and idioms. A novelist isn't a philologist or sociologist except incidentally. But he must always bear in mind just what resources of speech he has to draw from, and if he does limit himself, he should do so only because it makes his novel more effective.

And he should never be in the least influenced by literary fashion as by the consideration of what he considers to be saleable. If he writes about any group from poor whites in the South to poor blacks in Harlem it should be only because he is besottedly and drawingly compelled to write about them: he wants to put down on paper the way they talk because he never tires of hearing it.

The two examples I've chosen are rather hackneyed. The fashionable group at the moment—though this may be out of date by the time it's printed—is New York Jewish. That's fine—the Yiddish as detailed by Leo Rosten is gloriously expressive. I have a notion, though, that many novelists choose this group and its idiom because it's a bandwagon which will, they hope, carry them to high sales and movie rights. They should remember that sometimes bandwagons don't get you anywhere when they're other people's. It's best to start off your own.

Another working rule for dialogue is that it should be possible to discover from the dialogue alone what sort of person is speaking.

I apply this test to a passage from Anthony Powell's *A Buyer's Market:*

"As a matter of fact, I have been about very little this summer," he said, frowning. "I found I had been working a shade too hard, and had to—well—give myself a bit of a rest. . . . Then, the year before, I got jaundice in the middle of the season."

"Are you fit again now?"

"I am better. . . . But I intend to take care of myself. . . . My mother often tells me I go at things too hard. Besides, I don't really get enough air and exercise—without which one can never be truly robust."

"Do you still go down to Barnes and drive golfballs into a net?"

"Whenever feasible.". . . .

"Actually, one can spend too much time on sport if one is really going to get on. . . . And then I have my Territorials."

"You were going to be a solicitor when we last met."

"That would hardly preclude me from holding a Territorial officer's commission. . . ."

"Of course it wouldn't."

"I am with a firm of solicitors—Turnbull, Welford and Puckering, to be exact," he said. "But you may be sure that I have other interests too. Some of them not unimportant, I might add."[19]

The speaker here has a huge ego. He hasn't any sense of humour. He's obviously very pleased about his status as a professional man and speaks in the way he considers befitting to a professional man. To triumph over others, even though in a small way, gives him great pleasure. If there is any human warmth in his character, it isn't discernible.

And what my statement amounts to is no more than a collection of facts, and not even concrete facts. Even if they were expressed with more grace and precision or even wit, we wouldn't be shown a human being. Making statements isn't characterization, no matter how forcefully we make the statements. It's only when people speak that we know them.

But it isn't only by what they say and how they say it that we know them. Along with their speech we must detail their mannerisms, facial expressions or lack of facial expressions, their gestures, their physical state if relevant. Narrative and dialogue cannot be considered in separation. A novel isn't a play with detailed stage directions. Line by line your dialogue should be as speakable as stage dialogue, but it has to flow out of the narrative.

Nothing should be added to the dialogue unless it's necessary in order to make its meaning clear. For the way in which something is said may entirely alter its meaning. For example, "I'm sorry your dog is dead" means just that if the speaker has tears in his eyes. If he's smiling broadly, it means the exact opposite. And if a dog is to die in your novel, it's much more interesting if we know that the statement is accompanied by a smile.

Apart from this, too much straight dialogue can rapidly become tedious. Even if it's very good, there's always the problem of not being quite sure who's speaking. Whenever I as a reader come across a run of straight dialogue of much longer than a page, what I suspect as being the reason for it isn't artistic necessity but plain laziness. It's easier to write dialogue than narrative because narrative can be judged by set standards, even if only as prose. The only intention of dialogue is credibility, and this is a matter of opinion.

But, strangely enough, those who can't write credible dialogue can't write good prose either, and there is an inextricable relationship between the fact that Scott Fitzgerald writes superb narrative and superb dialogue. It isn't that the dialogue is merely an extension of his narrative. It could never be so, for its function is to give us words that we can accept as having been spoken in real life. But the same standards of craftsmanship apply to both.

I suspect that the reason that the ability to write good prose and good dialogue go hand-in-hand is simply that a good writer knows how to listen and is prepared to take infinite trouble.

But as a working rule, not more than one half of any novel should be dialogue. It isn't only that dialogue is easier to write—or seems easier to write—it's that the quotation marks have the effect of an authentic professionalism. They are, as it were, a guarantee that what's contained between them is actual speech. Once the quotation marks begin, the action appears to begin.

In fact, nothing at all has begun unless we remember from the outset two words of Henry James: Dramatize, dramatize. Every line of dialogue must advance the story, have conflict within it. Even when dialogue must be used to convey essential information, the information must have within it some element of surprise; it must be conveyed through the dialogue because this is the only possible way. And if information is to be conveyed through dialogue, it must be briefly.

"The bastard," said Tom. "I'll kill him, I swear to God I'll kill him." He looked as if he were going to vomit; his face was flushed and there were beads of sweat round his mouth and on his forehead. I put my hand on his arm. He was trembling violently. "Calm down. Who are you going to kill?"

The way you don't do it is to have Tom charge in, describe him, and then have him say: "I'll kill that bastard Travers. He's run off with Hilda. When I came home at six she'd gone and taken the kids. She left this note. . . ."
For once great dollops of information are ladled out, there is no drama, there is nothing to make us read on. Equally to be avoided is fake drama and the use of monosyllables.

"Calm down. Who are you going to kill?"
"You know."
"I don't."
"Travers."
"Not Travers!"
"Yes."

This sort of dialogue can extend a situation to two or three pages, or rather fill out two or three pages with the same effort that it would cost to fill half a page if the job were being done properly. There are, of course, times when a monosyllable can have shocking power, can reverberate through the whole book, can come between the reader and his sleep; but only on condition that the ground is prepared before hand, so that the monosyllable has crammed into it everything that has gone before.

It won't, incidentally, make this sort of dialogue any better if you attempt to build it up with descriptions of the way in which it's spoken:

"Yes." His voice had a dreadful finality.

For you really can't put very much expression into a monosyllable; expression depends upon timing, speed, rhythm, and emphasis, and no one can put these into a three-letter word. So make sure that all your stage directions work.

There is no need to put down everything which your characters would say in real life. Only put it down if it's essential to the story. Once you've established the speaker, once we've heard his authentic voice, then that's enough. Move to another speaker, or adapt the Raymond Chandler technique of having a man come into the room with a gun in his hand, or summarize. But the new voice has to be worth listening to, the new incident just as surprising as a man coming into the room with a gun in his hand, and the summary smooth and efficient. It should be far more than an abstract statement.

I will quote an example from my own novel, *Room at the Top*. Joe, the ex-sergeant, the working-class boy with a job at the Town Hall, is being put in his place by Brown, the rich industrialist, and his wife, and by Jack, the rich boyfriend of Brown's daughter. The problem was that to detail all that would be said would have taken about two thousand words. To put someone in his place, to impress upon him his inferior status, has to be done with some degree of finesse. If it's too blatant, it doesn't have the desired effect. But to have had two thousand words of dialogue at this point would have slowed up the pace which I wanted for the chapter. And a passage of dialogue of that kind, of that length, wouldn't have belonged to the novel.

John Braine

So I began with Jack speaking:

"By the way, weren't you at Compton Basset?" he asked.

"The Fifty-first," I said.

"A *very* great friend of mine was with that squadron. Darrow, Chick Darrow. Thoroughly decent chap, went to school with him. Went for a Burton over the Ruhr."

We noncoms used to say *got the chopper*. Going for a Burton was journalist's talk. It sickened me a bit, though I suppose that he was merely making an attempt to talk what he thought was my language. "I don't remember him."

"Oh, you must have met him. You couldn't miss old Chick. Bright red hair and a terrific baritone. Could've been professional."

"I never met him," I said, and kept saying for the next fifteen minutes during which he, assisted from time to time by Brown and his wife, played the Do You Know So and So game hard and fast from all angles, social, political, and even religious—they were *astounded* that I didn't know Canon Jones at Leddersford, he was very High of course but he was the only clergyman of any intellectual distinction whatever in the North of England. . . It's a well-known game, its object being the humiliation of those with less money than yourself; I wouldn't exactly say that they were successful in this, but I certainly paid dearly for Brown's whisky and the whisky which Jack also bought me. The extra refinement, the grace-note, was Jack's waving away of my offer to buy the drinks. ("No, no old boy, frightfully dear stuff this.")

I've never in all my life felt so completely friendless; I was at bay among the glasses of sherry and whisky, with the vicious little darts laden with the pride-paralysing curare of Do you know—? and Surely you've met—? and You must have come across—? thrown at me unceasingly. Susan said very little but I could see that she knew what

94

was going on. She would have helped me if she could but didn't possess the necessary experience or strength of character to do so.

I'd had two pints of old at the St Clair before I went into the dance; combined with four whiskies and my increasing irritation they made me forget my usual caution. I wasn't drunk; but I wasn't fully in control of myself. Jack asked me if I knew the Smiling Zombie's son.

"Amazing chap," he said. "Mind you, he'll kill himself in that old Alfa. Drives like a maniac. You must know him, he's always around Dufton."

"I don't know any tallymen," I said.

There was silence.

"I don't follow you, old man."

"A tallyman sells clothes on credit," I said. "In effect it's moneylending. You buy direct from the manufacturer and sell at a retail price about fifty per cent above what I, or any other person with eyes in his head, would pay. Then you charge interest—"

"It's business," Jack cut in. "You wouldn't refuse the profits, would you?"

"It's a dirty business," I said.[20]

The summary is, I hope, interesting because it's specific and because of the use of the metaphor of the Do You Know So and So game. I'm specific about time, too; what Joe is also saying is that there was an actual conversation and he's summarizing it. He remembers exactly how long it lasted because every minute lasted the full sixty seconds.

I don't, of course, say that this is the only way to do it. There are times when the summary need only be brief. But the reader should always be left with the feeling that you've been selective, that the words which are summarized have all actually been spoken, but you haven't put them down because they'd be boring.

How to portray a boring person is a different matter. This

must necessarily be done mainly through his conversation, since there is a limit to what you can write about his effect upon other people. You certainly can't do it through being strictly realistic: Apart from their habit of repetition, what makes bores boring is the simple fact that they talk too much. Your bores in that case would actually be boring, and to be boring is the one offence of which you must never be guilty. What you must do is to convey the essence of the bore's character—which is an overweening sense of his own importance and an almost complete lack of humour. (There are bores who imagine that they possess a sense of humour, and they're the worst bores of all.)

"As you probably know," he said, "my opinions have moved steadily to the left of late years. I quite see that there are aspects of Hitler's programme to which objection may most legitimately be taken. For example, I myself possess a number of Jewish friends, some of them very able men—Jimmy Klein, for example—and I should therefore much prefer that item of the National Socialist policy to be dropped. I am, in fact, not at all sure that it will *not* be dropped when matters get straightened out a bit. After all, it is sometimes forgotten that the National Socialists are not only 'national', they are also 'socialist'. So far as that goes, I am with them. They believe in planning. Everyone will agree that there was a great deal of the old Germany that it was right to sweep away—the Kaisers and Krupps, Hindenburgs and mediatized princes, stuff of that sort—we want to hear no more about them."[21]

Widmerpool isn't, of course, at all concerned whether his audience is interested in his opinions about Nazi Germany. He doesn't know anything about the realities of Nazi rule—he can't, because he has no imagination, another essential quality of the bore. He doesn't expect to be disagreed with, even when he finally makes a most fantastic suggestion:

"Take a man like Goering. Now, it seems pretty plain to me from looking at photographs of him in the papers that he only likes swaggering about in uniforms and decorations. I expect he is a bit of a snob—most of us are at heart—well, ask him to Buckingham Palace. Show him round. What is there against giving him the Garter? After all, it is what such things are for, isn't it?"[22]

And this is the heart of the matter. The bore is essentially comic; he is always unaware that he's lost his trousers and someone's painted his nose red.

A general note here about humour: No formula exists for the proportion of humour in your dialogue. But dialogue that is entirely serious, which doesn't contain at least some attempts at humour, is not only ultimately depressing, but also false. Not very many people are genuinely funny all the time, but the majority try to be funny some of the time. You don't have to introduce comic characters deliberately, you don't have to contrive comic incidents, but merely remember that most people say or hear at least one funny thing every day.

There remains the question of profanity and obscenity. It's hardly necessary to say that there isn't today any need for blanks or asterisks or euphemisms. Neither need you refer to "unprintable language" or a "torrent of obscenity." Put down the words which people actually use. But bear in mind that the majority of people use only a little mild profanity ("My God," but not "Christ") and that words like *bugger, crap, shit, piss, fart, prick, cock, cunt,* and *fuck* are mainly used in entirely masculine company. An interesting exception is their use in intellectual circles by both sexes.

I don't propose to discuss whether such words should be used or not; though very many good novelists have got along perfectly well without them. And of course a great deal depends upon the sort of people you're going to write about:

John Braine

There are many people, by no means prudish, who go through their whole lives without either hearing or using these words. My firm rule is the fewer the better, particularly with what are called four-letter words. This isn't for reasons of prudery. It's purely for artistic reasons. Four-letter words are words of power still; the less they're used, the more power they have to shock.

SIX: Narrative prose

My working rule with narrative prose is the same as for dialogue: If it can't be read aloud, it's no good. I don't mean by this that your narrative is supposed to represent actual speech. But your prose must have the rhythms of speech. Otherwise it becomes arid and obscure and intellectualized. It may, by any other test than the ear, be brilliant; but it won't do for a novel. For though it doesn't have to pretend to be otherwise than written, still, behind every novel is a man telling us a story face-to-face.

As I've said before, no one can teach you how to write a story. You can, however, be taught to write decent prose, which is simply clear and understandable prose. This doesn't necessarily mean absolutely bare prose. It doesn't mean that your prose can't be complex. It doesn't mean that you're not allowed metaphor. There are no limits to what you can do, to the tricks you can play with words, as long as you remember, in Flaubert's words, that if your prose doesn't follow the rhythms of the human lungs, then it isn't worth a damn. If you doubt this, then look at the prose of Shakespeare or Webster or Donne, which is very specifically meant to be spoken aloud.

Another rule—and I'm aware that it's a counsel of perfection—is to do without adjectives. If you do use one, let it be the least expected one. For when you eliminate adjectives, then you're forced to find the right verb and the right noun. Verbs and nouns together are naked and active;

the putting together of a noun and a verb means, as often as not, that you've used the first noun which came into your head, and that the noun could only be given colour and life by sticking on an adjective. The strength of English is its huge variety of synonyms; the word which expresses precisely the shade of meaning which you need is always there if you look for it. To reject adjectives means that you have no option but to look for it.

You must also reject clichés. They don't say anything and, in any case, are almost always used inaccurately. When something is described as being as white as snow, for example, the comparison is made without considering the fact that snow isn't always the same shade of white. And blood isn't always the same shade of red or grass the same shade of green. Describe the colour of a material as being the bright frothy red of arterial blood, and the cliché is no longer a cliché. To be exact, to take the trouble mentally to use one's five senses is to eliminate the cliché.

And that is all there is to metaphor. You take your images from your own experience, from the life around you. A metaphor isn't an ornament, a decoration attached to a plain statement. It's the only possible way of describing what you have to describe. This is most of all true when you're describing a state of mind:

I felt a certain reaction to what she said, but I am a slow-thinking man, and it occurred to me simultaneously that of all natural forces, vitality is the incommunicable one. In days when juice came into one as an article without duty, one tried to distribute it—but always without success; to further mix metaphors, vitality never "takes," You have it or you haven't it, like health or brown eyes or honour or a baritone voice. I might have asked some of it from her, neatly wrapped and ready for home cooking and digestion, but I could never have got it—not if I'd waited around for a thousand hours with the tin cup of self-pity. I could walk from her door, holding myself very carefully like cracked crockery, and go away into the world of bitterness, where I was making a home with such materials as are found there—and quote to myself after I left her door:

"*Ye are the salt of the earth. But if the salt hath lost its savour, wherewith shall it be salted?*"
Matthew 5-13.[23]

I've chosen this extract from Scott Fitzgerald's *The Crack-Up* because the writer's only concern here is to describe his personal situation. If he could have expressed himself by means of plain statement, he would have done so. But the words to express his state of mind don't exist. (Perhaps they exist in the vocabulary of psychology, but he wasn't a psychologist.)

Metaphor, for the creative writer, isn't an extension of language. It is almost another language. I'm even wrong to use the term "plain statement." If, paradoxically, metaphor isn't plain statement, then it fails. If it has no relevance to the story, then it fails. If it holds up the story, then it fails.

There are, of course, too many rules here to keep in the mind all at once. The overall rule in the writing of a novel is to keep it in the concrete, to avoid the abstract. All my rules have been taken from others; I have devised none myself. This rule for writing good prose was lifted straight from Stuart Chase's *The Tyranny of Words*.[24] This has been the most important book in my life. It isn't for me to say whether my work has any lasting merit, but if I have been able to make a living as a professional novelist, it has been entirely due to reading Chase's book at a formative age. Before I read it I knew that I wanted to write, but I didn't know what writing was about. I wanted to write well, but I didn't know how to set about learning how to write well. I wanted a style of my own, but I thought that style was a sort of conjuring trick.

John Braine

I believe that I had good natural taste; I divided novels in particular into dead and alive. I couldn't say why, and didn't realize that if I couldn't judge other people I couldn't judge myself. I'm sure that I believed in inspiration, that the ability to write would be given me without my taking any conscious thought about it. What saved me, what made me instantly grasp the truth of Chase's arguments, was that I have an essentially earth-bound mind and a devouring interest in the material world. Ideas mean nothing to me unless I can perceive their connection with the material world.

I shall not attempt to summarize Chase's book; you must read it for yourself. But its essence is the examination of the relationship between word and referent. The referent is

the object or situation in the real world to which the word or label refers. A beam of light comes from a moving animal to my optic nerve. The animal, which I recognize through prior experience with similar animals, is the referent. Presently I add the label and say, 'That's a nice dog.' Like the term 'semantics', I shall use the term 'referent' frequently in the following pages. Inded the goal of semantics might be stated as 'Find the referent.' When people can agree on the thing to which their words refer, minds meet. The communication line is cleared.[25]

Chase goes on to define three groups of words or, as he puts it, labels:

1. Labels for common objects, such as "dog", "chair", "pencil". Here difficulty is at a minimum.

2. Labels for clusters and collections of things, such as "mankind", "consumers' goods", "Germany", "the white race", "the courts". These are abstractions of a higher order, and confusion in their use is widespread. There is no entity "white race" in the world outside our heads, but only some millions of individuals with skins of an obvious or dubious whiteness.

3. Labels for essences and qualities, such as "the sublime", "freedom", "individualism", "truth". For such terms, there are no discoverable referents in the outside world, and by mistaking them for substantial entities somewhere at large in the environment, we create a fantastic wonderland. This zone is the especial domain of philosophy, politics, and economics.

We normally beg the hard question of finding referents and proceed learnedly to define the term by giving another dictionary abstraction, for example, defining "liberty" by "freedom"—"thus peopling the universe with spurious entities, mistaking symbolic machinery for referents." We seldom come down to earth, but allow our language forms or symbolic machinery to fashion a demonology of absolutes and high-order abstractions, in which we come to believe as firmly as Calvin believed in the Devil.[26]

As a novelist, your words should all come from the first group. (I am, of course, talking here specifically about narrative.) This is, of course, a counsel of perfection, as is dispensing with adjectives. But the test is simple: If you can't find a referent for the word, then you're writing nonsense. It might be splendid as philosophy but you're not a philosopher. It isn't your job to think in the abstract.

The test becomes second nature. So does the decision as to when it's not necessary to apply it—or, for that matter, possible. You can't really find any referents for thoughts, unless it's minute electrical charges. You can't really find any referents for states of mind like happiness or depression, or for qualities like good or evil. You can, however, present your character's thoughts exactly as you imagine that they really are, no matter how shocking or incongruous. Whether or not it's possible to find an absolutely accurate image for the state of mind, it is most definitely possible to describe exactly the circumstances of the person concerned; and if this is done properly, a simple statement is often enough. This is

irrespective of the correspondence of the circumstances to
the state of mind; as often as not, to choose a very simple
example, it's the contradiction of the circumstances by the
state of mind, as with someone feeling depressed on a fine
day, which describes the state of mind fully, but in only a few
words. The sun shines on and the birds sing through the
depression; fine day and depression are in the same world.
Let your main effort go into describing what you can describe.
All that matters is the physical world and what happens in it.

It was when I discovered *The Tyranny of Words* that I
ceased to worry about evolving an individual style. I had the
dim idea of creating something out of Hemingway, Joyce,
Lawrence, and Dos Passos; I even used to copy out passages
from them to imagine myself in their shoes, have some of
their talent rub off on me. I realized after reading *The Tyranny
of Words* that this was adolescent and egoistic. The function
of prose is to convey meaning to as many readers as possible.
Style, in the sense of being unmistakably oneself, is a
by-product. The more one consciously strives for it, the
further away one will go from it.

Along with the search for the referent came the growing
conviction that what the average reader didn't find easy to
read was bad prose. Rarely, if ever, bad because too clever,
too complex; but bad because not properly worked out, bad
because words were used without the author knowing what
they really meant. And so I drew up another childishly simple
working rule: Don't use any word if you're not sure about its
meaning.

At the same time—and as this book proceeds, the
contradictions mount up—you mustn't write down to your
audience, mustn't be afraid of the most complex constructions, recondite metaphors, the rarest words, as long as
they're the only ones which will express exactly what you
mean. I'm convinced—and again have only my instincts to

back me—that good writing can be understood and enjoyed even when words are used which aren't known to the general public. As long as you, the writer, know what they mean, the public will know.

I see as my audience everyone of average intelligence from sixteen onwards. Since at this age most children are capable of coping with Shakespeare and Chaucer and the New Mathematics, I see no reason why they shouldn't comprehend me. If I set my sights any lower, I shouldn't enjoy writing.

I shall not list the faults you should avoid because that would be merely negative. And I couldn't make the list comprehensive under forty-thousand words. Nor shall I state what is correct English usage: Sir Ernest Gowers and H. W. Fowler, among others, have done it for me. I can only make a general statement here: It's always better to be correct. Even if, to choose only one example, everyone else uses "decimate" as meaning reduction by nine-tenths, you must use it as meaning reduction by a tenth. I don't mean that you must be pedantic, but simply that you mustn't be sloppy.

The question still arises, after you've followed all my working rules, of how you can judge whether your prose is as good as it should be. One answer is that you don't ask yourself the question; ask yourself only functional, *working* questions—does my prose do what it has set out to do?

As long as you don't ask yourself about the merits of your prose, you'll be told the answer. Follow my rules—I realize how arrogant this claim must sound—and you'll be told not only about your prose, but about the novel itself.

This knowledge came to me with a passage in the last chapter of *Room at the Top:*

I ordered a bottle of IPA and a gin-and-it. Time was beginning to move too quickly, to slither helplessly away; each minute I looked at my watch it was ten minutes later; I knew that I'd only that minute met Mavis, but that minute was anything up to a year ago; as I drank the sharp summer-smelling beer the floor started to move again. Then every impression possible for one man to undergo all gathered together from nowhere like a crowd at the scene of an accident and yelled to be let in: time dancing, time with clay on its hobnailed boots, the new taste of the beer and the old taste of brandy and rum and fish and cornflour and tobacco and soot and wool scourings and Mavis' sweat that had something not quite healthy about it and her powder and lipstick—chalk, orris-root, pear-drops—and the hot hand of brandy steadying me again and just as it seemed that there wasn't to be any other place in the world but the long room with the green *art moderne* chairs and glass-topped tables, we were out in the street with our arms round each other's waists and turning in and out of narrow streets and alleys and courts and patches of waste ground and over a footbridge with engines clanging together aimlessly in the cold below as if slapping themselves to keep warm and then we were in a corner of a woodyard in a little cave of piled timber; I took myself away from my body, which performed all the actions she expected from it. She clung to it after the scalding trembling moment of fusion as if it were human, kissing its drunken face and putting its hands against her breasts.

There were houses very near on the dirt road at the top of the woodyard; I could hear voices and music and smell cooking. All around were the lights of the city; Birmingham Road rises from the centre of Leddersford and we were on a little plateau about halfway up; there was no open country to be seen; not one acre where there wasn't a human being, two hundred thousand separate lonelinesses, two hundred thousand different deaths. And all the darkness the lights had done away with, all the emptiness of fields and woods long since built over, suddenly swept over me, leaving no pain, no happiness, no despair, no hope, but simply nothingness, the ghost in the peepshow vanishing into the blank wall and no pennies left to bring him out again.[27]

The answer came with the sentence beginning "And all the darkness. . . ." I knew when I read it over that my prose was the best that I could do, that it presented my characters and my world with absolute clarity. The novel all hung together, it was a unity. But I can't put into words exactly what I felt, except, quite simply, that I knew that it would be all right.

This moment only comes once, and it can come at any point in the book. It cannot be induced by any means, and it's best not to hope for it. To have its possibility in your mind is almost to scare it away. It will inform you that you're going in the right direction or that you have gone in the right direction. I won't tell you how to recognize it because I can't. But you can't mistake it; there is no other experience to match it.

SEVEN: First- and third-person narrative

I shall now examine the two main narrative viewpoints, first and third person. To a great extent, this is a matter of personal temperament. You still must consider the advantages and disadvantages of each viewpoint and its variations, but by no means go against your instincts. It is, of course, possible to write two different versions of the same novel, but some freshness will be lost with the second version. Or you can use both viewpoints in the same novel, but I don't recommend this. It's too complicated.

The advice generally given in books of this nature is to use the third person. The first person is said to have too many limitations, since everything obviously must happen before the eyes of the narrator. There's the danger of its becoming autobiographical or being considered autobiographical by the reader. And the narrator tends to be a shadowy figure; there are some critics who assert that a first-person hero can't be a memorable character.

Despite this, I strongly recommend that your first novel should be in the first person. Whilst you must never avoid what is difficult out of laziness, it doesn't make sense not to take the easiest way if, provably, it works. And first-person narrative works. It's entirely natural to buttonhole your audience and tell them of all the interesting things which happened to you personally. The use of the first person gives your tale veracity. *You* know all the details because *you* were there; you tell the story because it happened to *you*. You can, of course, tell a story in the first person about someone else. But if you do this, there is a danger that artificiality can creep in. To tell a story about someone else is in fact only natural when that person is intimately involved with us. It isn't that it can't be done, as in *The Great Gatsby,* but I wouldn't recommend it for your first novel.

There is the question of the dangers of autobiography. This is avoided by the very simple expedient of not telling your own life-story and, above all, not making the narrator a writer or an artist of any kind.

There is time enough to worry about the reviewers' reactions when the book is published. However, you should be forewarned. Almost certainly some will be simpleminded enough to object to the hero *not* being a novelist on the grounds that only a novelist could be so competent a narrator. (They thus manage to hand out adverse criticism and praise in the same breath.) Some are even more simpleminded and assume that you must be the hero. You need take no notice of this. The convention of first-person narrative is that the fact of the narrator being fully articulate is no part of his character. No one must comment upon his being articulate or upon his keenly observing everything around him. He's telling his story, but as the storyteller he's a different person from the person in the story. And he mustn't make any comments about the mechanics of the story. He can say that there are some parts of it he doesn't want to remember, for instance, but he can't comment on his use of literary devices. The best working rule here is for him never to use any word or phrase which indicates that he is writing the story. He is remembering, which is absolutely different.

Do not attempt what Mary McCarthy calls the impersonation trick. Don't pretend to be someone completely out of the range of your experience. To make your narrator someone like yourself is not to be autobiographical. And don't try to give the impression of someone actually speaking, don't use dialect or any kind of argot. It comes off in Anthony Burgess' *A Clockwork Orange,* and in Keith Waterhouse's *There Is a Happy Land,* but I don't know of any others. Again, don't make things unnecessarily difficult for yourself. Don't put yourself in the position where every word of your narrative is an effort and where you can use virtually none of your own experience. Remember that as long as you tell the truth, you'll be original, even shockingly so.

It is one of the strengths of the first person that for the narrator to be completely honest has far more impact than when you're describing his thoughts in the third person. This is another advantage of the first person: You depict the main character's thoughts absolutely naturally. When someone is telling you a story in real life, you take it for granted that he'll tell you his thoughts. But if he were telling you about a third person's, that would be completely unnatural. When thoughts are at variance with spoken words, you're let into a secret, and the story is given an additional twist:

"Are you enjoying the show?" I asked Susan.

"It's *gorgeous.* I adore ballet. And the music—it makes me feel all *squashy* inside—I feel, oh, ever so excited and squiffy." She put her elbow on the table and cupped her chin in her hand. "It's ever so difficult to explain . . . it's like being inside a house all painted with beautiful colours and when you listen it's like touching the paint, the colours all run over your mind—does that sound silly?"

"No. Not one little bit. I've always felt like that myself, only I can't put it as well as you." I was lying, of course; as far as I'm concerned ballet is something with which to occupy the eyes whilst listening to music. But I wouldn't have dreamed of saying so; it was essential that I should appear to share Susan's interests—or rather, that they should appear to coincide. I'd discover something unimportant to disagree with her about so that she'd think me an intelligent type with a mind of my own.[28]

This is how the relationship with Susan, the rich man's daughter, is always going to be. Joe is never honest with her; he's always calculating the effect of everything he says. He's being quite honest in another sense, though; he's admitting what he really thought.

I don't think that it matters that we aren't told what Susan is thinking. We can judge by her words and behaviour; we're in the same position as Joe. He knows in the end, when she allows herself to be seduced by him, that his campaign has been successful; in any case, as with a surprising number of people, there's no great gap between her words and her thoughts.

This is only one approach. It is possible to write a novel in the first person and not deal with the narrator's thoughts at all. This is absolutely legitimate. For I most emphatically don't mean that you should attempt to write a novel like mine. But if you set down in full what you say and what you think in the space of only one hour, then what will be revealed, unless you're a saint or a simpleton, will be a seething mass of contradictions, lies, half-truths, generosity mixed with calculation, love with lust, arrogance with timidity—we have every kind of impulse and mood within us, none of us is ever consistent. But honesty works two ways: You mustn't soft-pedal your narrator's decent impulses. And if, for instance, he's praised for good behaviour or outstanding achievement, he hasn't got to be modest about it within his thoughts, whatever motions of self-deprecation he may go through on the exterior.

This, too, is something you must be prepared for: There is actually a school of thought which holds that characters must be consistent and that your feelings about them must be

John Braine

consistent. It need only be said that this is dangerous rubbish, for no one is consistent. Bear in mind always that in his *persona* as narrator your character has no shame whatever and no desire to present himself in a good light. This is another convention which has to be accepted.

Whatever happens when the narrator isn't there should preferably reach him in the form of dialogue as it would in real life. The message will be fragmentary, put together by deduction and guesswork. You shouldn't stop the story, as it were, whilst another character tells his story at length. Nor should overmuch use be made of summary. The ball should at all times be kept in the narrator's court. It's his voice we should hear; when we hear others it should be only in relation to him.

Summary can, of course, be used quite naturally in the first person. In fact, not to use it, either at certain points to continue narrating directly, or to cut, would be either tedious or all too smooth and literary. One way or the other, the impression of a man telling us a story at his ease would have gone.

Unless one is to adapt the very difficult course of observing all the unities, of covering a short period in time in full detail, there must be in any story periods of time during which nothing in particular happens.

There was music from my neighbour's house through the summer nights. In his blue garden men and girls came and went like moths among the whisperings and the champagne and the stars. At high tide in the afternoon I watched his guests diving from the tower of his raft, or taking the sun on the hot sands of his beach while his two motor-boats slit the waters of the Sound, drawing aquaplanes over cataracts of foam. On week-ends his Rolls-Royce became an omnibus, bearing parties to and from the city between nine in the morning and long past midnight, while his station wagon

112

scampered like a brisk yellow bug to meet all trains. And on Mondays eight servants, including an extra gardener, toiled all day with mops and scrubbing-brushes and hammers and garden-shears, repairing the ravages of the night before.

Every Friday five crates of oranges and lemons arrived from a fruiterer in New York—every Monday these same oranges and lemons left his back door in a pyramid of pulpless halves. There was a machine in the kitchen which could extract the juice of two hundred oranges in half an hour if a little button was pressed two hundred times by a butler's thumb.

At least once a fortnight a corps of caterers came down with several hundred feet of canvas and enough coloured lights to make a Christmas tree of Gatsby's enormous garden. On buffet tables, garnished with glistening hors-d'oeuvre, spiced baked hams crowded against salads of harlequin designs and pastry pigs and turkeys bewitched to a dark gold. In the main hall a bar with a real brass rail was set up, and stocked with gins and liquors and with cordials so long forgotten that most of his female guests were too young to know one from another.[29]

This doesn't only cover a period of time when the narrator tries to sell bonds and sort out his life generally. In addition it tells us how Gatsby lives. It also makes clear the position of the narratur—on the outside, looking in. This is not his world. He will be involved with it; he will never be drawn in by it. None of this is stated directly. It is all observation of a mode of life which isn't that of the majority. As an experiment, imagine yourself in the narrator's shoes and put the paradox in your own words—"Nothing very much happened during the next few weeks. But Gatsby kept on having these terrific parties—you wouldn't believe it, you wouldn't really—"

The Great Gatsby was, of course, the achievement of maturity. In a way, it's a difficult example to follow. In *Room at the Top* I do much the same kind of thing rather more obviously:

> I spent Christmas at my Aunt Emily's. It snowed in Warley the night I left, just a light powdering, a present from Raphael's and Tuck's and Sharpe's to make the girls' eyes sparkle and the waits sing in tune and to turn the houses taller and crookeder and all's-well-in-the-end adventurous; the town was crammed with people, all of them none the less absolute tenants of happiness because they'd been shepherded into it by the shop-keepers and the newspapers and the BBC: you could sense that happiness innocent and formal as a children's story, with each snowflake and each note of the Town Hall carillon.
>
> It was hard to leave Warley then; I felt as if I were being sent home from a party before the presents had been taken off the tree. In fact, I'd felt out of things all December: I'd gone to the Thespians' Christmas party, and been the back end of a horse in the children's play, and kissed all the girls at the Town Hall after the traditional lunchtime boozeup, but I knew that I wasn't part of Warley's festival, because I was leaving before the preparations began to make sense, before that short turkey and spice-cake and wine and whisky period when every door in the town would be wide open and the grades wouldn't matter. Not that I really believed such a thing could happen; but in Warley it at least was possible to dream about it.[30]

There was no alternative. I do state quite explicitly that nothing of any consequence was happening at this time, but I also reiterate what Joe feels about Warley. What he feels about Warley is the subject of the passage, not that nothing very much was happening. I can't tell exactly how I'd have dealt with the problem if the novel had been in the third person, but it certainly wouldn't have been in the form of summary. A working rule here—childishly simple as always—is that a summary whould always have some other purpose besides its most obvious one. This secondary purpose should appear the primary purpose. But if it really were the primary purpose, if Fitzgerald had no other aim in mind but to give the narrator's view of Gatsby's parties, or I had only concerned myself with a reiteration of Joe's feelings about Warley, then the story would have become static; it would be a series of stills and not a film.

As for a first-person narrator being necessarily a shadowy character, I don't think that this is the case with the narrator of *Room at the Top*. Unless you follow the weird convention that the narrator has to be a thoroughly decent chap—a convention by which most reviewers, no matter how progressive their views, seem to believe all novelists should be bound—then I don't see how the form itself can affect the characterization. Another convention, which you should note, is to make the hero, whether the narrator or not, a loser. This tradition of the novel is that, as Cyril Connolly remarks, the hero has the dirt done on him by life, his symbol is the sad clown Petrouchka. That's fine, if that's what you want, but do ask yourself if you don't prefer the outrageously unstoppable Punch.

There is a variation of the first-person narrative in which there is more than one narrator. I don't recommend this because it's too complicated and episodic. I can accept the one voice telling me his story and, over the space of eighty thousand words or so, get to know him as a person. But—and I know this is a purely subjective reaction—I can't accept the different people being trotted on; somewhere I see a puppet-master.

The third-person narrative in its simplest form concentrates upon the hero. We don't see anything that he wouldn't see; he's there all the time. *Saturday Night and Sunday Morning*

John Braine

uses this form; it has the obvious merit of concentrating our interest and keeping the story moving, since we never know anything that the hero doesn't know. We never can know fully his effect on the lives of other people nor see them as fully as we see him; he's the only one in the round, so to speak. But we still know the other characters as well as he knows them, which is as well as we know anyone in real life. The great advantage is a clear story-line which always goes forward: Once you begin to look at other characters as fully as at the hero, you begin to have problems of time. Going backwards and forwards in time from one character to another and one viewpoint to another can lead the reader to the stage where he doesn't know what's happening. It can also lead him to the stage where surprise follows surprise, where complexity is a delight, a mirror of the complexity of life.

But with your first novel it's best not to attempt more than you can perform. In the arts there are no A's awarded for effort. You will not be condemned for taking the easiest—or rather the least difficult—way. All that matters is to have your novel published. Let the complexity and the mystery be within your characters. The less time you have to give your method of narration, the more you have to give to your characters and your story—and, as I've already said, you can't separate one from the other.

I personally didn't feel ready to deal with more than one character in depth until my sixth novel, *The View from Tower Hill*. Whether I was successful or not isn't for me to say. But I didn't feel able to handle this method of narration until I'd had considerable experience. As a professional writer I can't afford to make the wrong decision. I don't have the time: There are too many books I want to write before I die.

And neither do you have the time to waste. Use any other form of narration but straight first- or third-person and you'll be wasting your time. You may even risk a worse fate than rejection, which is not to finish the novel. Nothing diminishes more talent than unfinished work; nothing diminishes more the will to try again. Even rejection is preferable.

EIGHT: The point of improbability

There is, of course, no sure way of pleasing the public. It should theoretically be possible for any person with narrative ability to devise a formula which would produce best-sellers. The proof that no such formula exists is the extremely small number of best-sellers in relation to the total of novels published.

On the whole, best-sellers aren't found among what I'll call, for the sake of convenience, straight novels. Most people read for escape. So the thriller—which comprises spy stories, detective stories, and adventure stories—has the best chance of making a great deal of money for its author. Then there is the historical novel and its offshoot, the family saga. From the point of view of sales, the longer the better: The readers who want to escape into the past want to do it thoroughly. Successful historical novels and family sagas are seldom less than one hundred and fifty thousand words, successful thrillers seldom longer than one hundred thousand words.

Westerns, what are called light romances, and science fiction, generally have assured but moderate sales; those writers who make a living from them generally do so through sheer output.

Of one thing I'm certain: As Rebecca West said a long time ago, the Tosh Horse is never ridden with the tongue in the cheek. The real best-sellers represent the best that their authors can do. Being human, they ardently desire to make a lot of money, but money isn't what makes them write. They wouldn't be interested in making more money doing something else. And most of them are almost absurdly prolific even though punitive taxes make it unprofitable.

There is no best-selling formula; there is a common denominator of best-sellers. It is a well-constructed story. Every line must have a hook planted to lead the reader on to the next, every chapter must end with a surprise, a predicament, a big hook. The end must be a true end; all the book must be epitomized in the last paragraph. It must be what the book has been aiming towards, the target it has been planned to hit. The novel mustn't simply end because the author has run out of ideas; it mustn't end vaguely:

> Through the open window came the smell of wood-smoke. It had turned cooler now and the sky was reddening in the west. The room was very quiet. Ricky took Lorna's letter out of his pocket and looked at it with trembling hands. He put it down on the table; it still didn't seem possible for it all to end like this. Norman tapped out his pipe on the grate.
> "I don't know," he said, "I really don't know. Perhaps we made the wrong decision. Maybe it was *she* who was in the right. . . . God help me, I really don't know. . . ."

This is off the cuff, but it's an accurate representation of the way in which most English novels end. Their American counterparts would, I expect, have the hero get into his car and drive on through the night with no clear idea of his destination. Along with a vague end comes a disregard of loose threads. An end isn't satisfactory unless it ties them all up. All questions must be answered, or else the story cannot be said to have finished. It's better to do the job absolutely without artifice, brusquely and hurriedly, than not to do it at all.

To give examples of beginnings is, I think, legitimate because when choosing books one looks at the beginning; it's the shop window for all to see. But the ending is a different matter: We don't look at that because it would spoil our enjoyment of the story. So I shall quote no examples of endings, but instead shall recommend in particular that you look closely at the end of *The Great Gatsby, Appointment in Samarra,* and *The End of the Affair.* The standards to which you aspire must be no lower.

In the kind of novel which I write myself and which I'm trying to show you how to write, the story cannot be separated from the characters. The story is, from the moment of conception, the actions of the characters. I can't give you a formula for devising exciting plots, though I believe that such formulas do exist. In a sense you shouldn't notice the plot: It's what the characters do that you're interested in. And whatever they do should be completely credible.

Here comes the great difficulty. However appropriate the actions of your characters are, however solid their background, you're telling a story. You're planting the hooks to pull the reader on; you're directing the narrative to its culmination. You're presenting real human beings. But the story is still an artificial creation. Nothing in real life is ever neat and ordered, there are no real endings, the threads are left untied.

What you're trying to do, in fact, is the equivalent of what is done when the world, which is a sphere, is projected on a flat surface. The two entities are completely different. There must always be inaccuracy somewhere, some part of the world incorrectly represented in area and shape. And with the novel what one has to accept is what I term the Point of Improbability. If there is to be a well-constructed story, then somewhere, because of the needs of the story, something will happen which couldn't possibly happen in real life. Get rid of it, substitute a credible happening, and the Point of Improbability will pop up somewhere else.

There isn't any way of getting rid of it; to attempt to sneak quietly past it by means of a brief summary makes the incredible even more credible. The best way of dealing with it is with the maximum of brio; make sure that no one misses it. It almost always emerges at a time when a steady narrative pace has been established; to keep up this pace is vital, but at the Point of Improbability it must be slowed down, for it takes extra time to make a set piece. (The degree of effort never varies.)

This is the great distinction between the thriller and the straight novel. There is nothing that I have said about the straight novel which cannot be applied to the thriller except this. It isn't merely that there are more Points of Improbability in the thriller. A thriller won't be a thriller if it concerns itself about credibility. That is, as far as the story is concerned. The details, the background, the timetable, must be meticulously planned. We don't want to be told; we want to be shown exactly. We want to know about the kind of gun, the kind of knife, the meals eaten, the journeys taken, the physical appearance of every character. We don't want ever to be in any doubt as to when anything happened; part of the pleasure, as for example in Frederick Forsyth's *The Day of the Jackal*, is to be told the day, the date, and the hour. And we want real cities and towns and villages, real hotels and shops and public places; we're going to put ourselves into the hero's shoes; we're reading for escape, and to use places that we have visited ourselves or are able to visit makes that escape authentic, augments the fantasy.

And, above all, if people are killed, they must be really dead. Examine this passage from Donald Hamilton's *Death of a Citizen*.

I went back into the bathroom, set the shotgun by the door, rolled up my shirt sleeves, and bent over Barbara Herrera. It was time to get rid of some of the finer and more

121

sensitive feelings I'd developed since the war. I wanted to know precisely how she'd died; from the front she showed no marks of violence. I found a swelling at the side of her head, and a bullet-hole in back; her long hair and the back of her white dress were bloodsoaked. It wasn't hard to read the signs. She'd been taken by surprise, knocked out and carried into the bathroom, placed in the tub where the mess could easily be cleaned up later, and shot to death with a small-caliber pistol, the sound of which would have been barely audible through the thick adobe walls.

I thought I knew whose pistol had been used, and my guess was confirmed when I saw a little .22 caliber shell under the lavatory. It almost had to be from my gun; Tina went in for those little European pocket pistols with the calibers expressed in millimeters, and Frank Loris didn't look like a precision marksman to me. If he carried a gun at all, it would be something that would knock you down and walk all over you, like a .375 or .44 Magnum. It looked as if they were setting me up for something very pretty, or at least making quite certain of my cooperation, I reflected; and then, as I eased the dead girl gently back to her former position, I felt something between her shoulders, something hard and businesslike and unbelievable beneath the stained material of her dress.

Very much surprised, I checked my discovery. The outline was unmistakable, although I'd only met a rig like that once before. I didn't bother to pull the bloody dress down to get at it. I knew by feel what I'd find. It would be a flat little sheath holding a flat little knife with a kind of pear-shaped symmetrical blade and maybe a couple of thin pieces of fiber-board riveted on to form a crude handle. The point and edges would be honed, but not very sharp, because you don't make throwing knives of highly tempered steel unless you want them to shatter on impact.

It wouldn't be much of a weapon—a quick man could

duck it and a heavy coat would stop it—but it would be right there when someone pointed a gun at you and ordered you to raise your hands or, even better, clasp them at the back of your neck. Slide a hand down inside the neckline of your dress, under that long, black, convenient hair, and you were armed again. And there can be situations when even as little as five inches of not very sharp steel flickering through the air can make all the difference in the world.[31]

You'll note the calm expert way in which the hero examines the corpse. Also that the knife which he finds is fully described. In his profession, finding a corpse in the bathroom is all in the day's work; he doesn't, as the overwhelming majority of readers would do, throw up, then faint. The details aren't, so to speak, for the reader. The hero must know why the girl has been killed in order to carry out his mission and to stay alive, and he can't know why until he knows how.

But really it's all a confidence trick. The packaging is perfect. It's what's inside that doesn't bear close examination. This doesn't mean that I don't enjoy thrillers myself, and in particular Donald Hamilton's. I'm quite willing to suspend disbelief in order to get my ration of escape. But if you're interested in thrillers as a writer, you have to be able to distinguish between packaging and contents; you have to admit that you're a con man.

In the first instance, of course, no one is quite as ruthless, brave, tough, or lucky as Donald Hamilton's Matt Helm or Ian Fleming's James Bond or, in fact, any secret agent you can name. No Western Secret Service or Secret Service department is as efficient and callous and unscrupulous as those in fiction. The Le Carré-Deighton convention of our lot being as bad as the enemy is a confidence trick too. I don't really know anything about the Secret Service from the inside, but I suspect that in reality it's like most Western government departments—overstaffed, slow-moving, hemmed in by rules and regulations, but nevertheless functioning tolerably well. I also suspect that these days the secret agent's job is more likely to be concerned with organization and electronics than with Berettas and flat little knives with pear-shaped symmetrical blades. I further suspect that no private person or organization has a nuclear rocket base and that there aren't any secret superweapons. I already know that there aren't any supermen. Nor—and this is merely a cunning variation of the con trick—any secret agents quite so dingy and neurotic as the heroes of Le Carré and Deighton.

To write a thriller, you begin with improbability. Once the packaging is perfect, once the research has been done, then your only concern is to keep the story moving. The hero must always be in danger. He must at least once be helpless in the hands of the enemy, and he must escape. It's often been remarked that this is the most glaring improbability of all, since what happens to secret agents in the power of a ruthless enemy is that they're tortured for information, then killed.

But there are other improbabilities. Take, for instance, the most efficiently organized thriller, Frederick Forsyth's *The Day of the Jackal.* When examined, the whole plot will be seen to depend upon two improbabilities. The first is that an OAS member, whose god is his commanding officer, would leave his post without telling him, would have any problem that he wouldn't take to him. The next is that a senior member of the French government, fully conversant with all the President's movements and security arrangements, wouldn't have had his phone tapped. (It is irrelevant whether at that time such a person would have his phone tapped; all that is relevant is what the reader will accept.) Once the phone is tapped, toward the end, the source of the leak of the measures being taken to trap the Jackal, hired by the OAS to assassinate the President, is discovered. There's a final twist, a final cliff-hanger, and it's all up with the Jackal.

The two major Points of Improbability each had an essential function. With the first, the assassination attempt and the code name of the assassin is revealed, and the hunt begins. Without the second, there would have been no story; the source of the leak would have been fed false information which would have led the Jackal into a trap. Come to that, there is yet another Point of Improbability: The information he needs comes to the Jackal via the senior official's mistress, who is by reason of her background an OAS sympathizer. Wouldn't there have been exhaustive surveillance of all the officials concerned in the security arrangements for De Gaulle?

Now, for an exercise, try to devise a plot which won't contain these Points of Improbability. For that matter, in case you're under the misapprehension that I'm denigrating the author, try to devise a plot which will maintain the interest of the reader unflaggingly despite the fact that he knows the ending before he's even begun. The author is deliberately throwing away the main ingredient of suspense. Whatever happens in the end, no matter how near the Jackal comes to success, we know that De Gaulle wasn't assassinated. And yet there are enormous gains. We're on the author's side: A sporting challenge has been issued. He'll keep us chewing our nails right to the end, even though, strictly speaking, there's nothing to chew our nails about. And there's an enormous increase in authenticity. We can believe in an unsuccessful attempt to assassinate De Gaulle, as we can't really believe in organizations like SPECTRE. We can believe in professional assassins like the Jackal as we can't believe in super-criminals like Goldfinger and Dr. No and Blofeld. And the OAS, which hires the Jackal, is, or was, a fact.

There is one important part of the novelist's craft which every successful thriller-writer and, indeed, every best-seller, virtually never skimps. As often as not the writer of what, wincing slightly, I'll call the serious novel does skimp it. The reason is, I'm convinced, sheer laziness. It's difficult to give a name to what I mean, precisely because the writing of novels is an art and not a science. There are no rules about what you put in and what you leave out. It may be essential to the story to chronicle fully an incident which on the face of it isn't essential to the story. It may be absolutely right, on the other hand, to deal with a key event in a few casual words of conversation. There are in writing a novel an unlimited number of options: Instinct is your only reliable guide as to which to take.

The best way to put it is this: If the reader is dissatisfied, if he hasn't been told about something he wanted to be told about, if the narrative has caused him to ask a question which hasn't been answered, then this is due to a deficiency in craftsmanship—or rather, as I have said, simply to laziness. And I'm somehow sure that the writer is always aware when he's been guilty of this offence. His instincts, if he really is a novelist, tell him that he should write the scene in question; but such scenes always present a problem. It's as if they were especially for the reader, and the other scenes were just for oneself. Or so one rationalizes it. The truth is that the scenes one leaves out are more explanatory than dramatic; the problem is how to make them readable, how to keep the impact of the story.

Mr. Irving Wallace is by any definition a best seller. I'm not being supercilious when I say that it's highly unlikely that any of his novels will be regarded as great literature. His existence is scarcely noticed by the critics, and is never likely to be. But he is a conscientious craftsman who works hard and who gives the public value for money. He is a best seller simply because he tells a good story—and because his novels are filled out, because they answer all the reader's questions.

In *The Writing of One Novel* he deals with this matter of evasion of the difficult. After publishing a best-seller, he realized that he was avoiding the big subject:

I had been thinking about the Nobel novel off and on, as always, and then late in 1959 I saw fully, all at once, what I had refused to see before but what I must finally come to grips with and overcome. I realized that until then I had always been afraid of doing the big central story. While I had promising fictional characters in mind, I had avoided the real challenge of the subject itself. I had walked around and around it, which was safer. For only when you are fully engaged can you fail—in your own eyes or the world's eyes—as often as succeed. I had not wanted to chance the failure apparently. Or perhaps I had been fearful of pitting my untried resources against so monstrously frightening a test. In my earlier outlines I had been ready to undertake only small hells, never the big one.[32]

This is something to be thought about, and the fact that Mr. Wallace isn't going to figure in the literary histories doesn't diminish the value of his reflections. But from there he goes on to reflect about the matter of evasion of the difficult scene.

I have since found that this fear is common among writers not only when attacking an overall subject but when facing up to a single scene inside a novel. Too many authors will avoid what threatens to be an impossibly difficult scene, although an obligatory scene, and instead will write around it rather than into it, simply from fear that they do not possess the perception or skill to master it. This detour into exposition or past tense or summary, as substitute for daring to dramatise or play out a crucial confrontation, may be entirely unconscious. But once the fear is understood, and once the work in progress dominates the writer and drives him into the big Hell, the author has a chance to live up to his potential. He may be bad before he is good, but one day he will be good, or as good as he can ever be.[33]

This is a professional speaking; his literary status is

127

irrelevant. I shall only say that if you avoid the difficult, whether the difficult subject or the difficult scene, then you'll not only not progress as a writer, but will actually decline, even dry up. It isn't merely a matter of having a greater chance of commercial success, but a matter of using your talent to its fullest. The more that is asked from talent, the more it gives.

One of the besetting faults of the first novelist is lack of variety of scene. The drawing room, the pub, and the bedroom have a fatal attraction. Dialogues tend to be duologues. It is, again, a question of avoiding what is difficult. But to limit oneself in one's choice of backgrounds is to throw away the chief advantage of the novelist. There is no limit to the number of backgrounds, just as there is no limit to the number of characters. You don't have a budget to keep within; you don't have to worry about the weather for outdoor locations. Oddly enough, most first novelists limit themselves far more in their choice of scene than do writers for television. The first thing one learns in television is the necessity of variety in background.

For a story, if it is to convince us, doesn't take place in a vacuum. Our behaviour is influenced and our character revealed by the place which we're in. It isn't enough to be shown our characters only in their leisure hours; we must also see them at work.

About three months after their work in Louisiana was completed Hasbrouck sent for Alfred. "I'm not going to beat about the bush," said Hasbrouck. "How much do you want for your options on that Louisiana land?"

"I don't know. You must know something I don't know."

"We do. Mr. MacHardie should be handling this himself, but I have a sneaking suspicion he wants me to eat crow, and I'm prepared to do that. I was wrong, and you were right. There's oil. How much, we don't yet know. Now you can raise the money to finance additional investigation yourself, if you like. Or you can sell us your options at a considerable profit and we'll develop the property if there's anything there."

"*If* there's anything there?"

"There's oil there, but we don't know that it's one of the great pools, or just one of those freaks. And I have been asked to tell you that your decision in no way affects your job here. That's up to you."

"Will you give me some time to think about it?"

"Take a week, if you like. Go down to Louisiana and find out what you can. This firm will be here when you get back."

"I didn't mean a week. I meant a couple of minutes," said Alfred. He watched Hasbrouck's effort to retain his composure, turning a long gold pencil over and over, running his fingers down the pencil to the bottom, then up-ending it and starting again at the top. Hasbrouck had well-manicured hands and his cuffs were starched, and hands and cuffs became symbols of the man in the present situation: whatever was going on inside him, he was not showing it. He had spoken of eating crow, but he had displayed no humility or even respect, and yet Alfred sensed that if he gave an answer that was unsatisfactory to the firm, Hasbrouck would resign. Months might pass, but only to enable Hasbrouck, and indirectly the firm itself, to save face.

"All right, Mr. Hasbrouck," said Alfred. "I've decided. I'll sell the options for $250,000 and one condition."

"What is the condition?"

"That the first well you bring in be called the Jack Rawlings."

"Now let's understand each other. You sell us the options—us will be a company we'll form, of course—for $250,000. That ends your participation in the deal?"

"Yes. That, and the naming of the first well."

"That's satisfactory. Congratulations. I think you showed great good sense. You didn't ask for too much money, you didn't gamble $250,000, which is what you'd been doing, you know. And you did nothing, I may say, to jeopardize your position with the firm. I'll tell you now that you made a very good guess. If you had asked for more than three hundred thousand, you wouldn't have got it. And regardless of our good intentions and our sincerity, I don't think you'd have been very happy here. Now tell me, please, why did you decide to risk $250,000 of your own money for those options? Do you know why?"

"I think I do. The old man trusted me, and he was a human being. I had no reason to trust him, but he trusted me. I'm almost sure to lose by it sometime, but I'd rather lose by it than hurt somebody who did trust me. Hard to explain."

"Well, we'll see that his name is perpetuated, or at least that's what we hope."

"Now I'd like to ask a question if I may. How do you know there's oil on that property?"

"You may ask, but I'm not at liberty to tell you. I *am* at liberty to tell you one thing you may have overlooked. If you'll read your contract with the firm, re-read it, you'll notice that there's a clause in it that covers just such a situation as this. Technically, under your contract, you *had* to sell us that property, and we didn't have to pay you a cent more than $250,000."

"I knew that, Mr. Hasbrouck."

"Oh, you did, did you?" For the first time there was some respect in Hasbrouck's smile, and that much respect remained there permanently. [34]

This extract from John O'Hara's *From the Terrace* shows how it has to be done. The sense of authenticity is overwhelming. We're eavesdropping on reality, we're being shown how the big money is made, a secret is being revealed. There is no vagueness about the details. The author hasn't made it up; he is reporting. But the drama isn't as much in the size of the payment for the options as in the choices which Alfred has to make. The deal isn't as simple as it looks. It can go wrong in several ways and upon it hangs now only his future with the firm but Hasbrouck's. Hasbrouck is in a sense at Alfred's mercy. But there's a twist in the end: What Alfred bases his decision to acquire the options on is his judgement of the character of the seller; and what eventually makes his huge profit possible is his judgement of the characters of the principals of his firm and their notion of business honour.

Analyzed in this way it all seems obvious; but it would be very easy to bungle it. It would have been bungled, it would have been dead, if it had been written to show the injustice of an economic system through which more than most people earn in a lifetime can be made in five minutes. It would have been dead if it had been written as background information, to show us how Alfred spent his working hours. But this part of Alfred's life is as important to the story as the part which he spends with his wife and mistress and friends and children.

There are, indeed, many men to whom work is the most important part of their lives. My personal impression is that American novels far more often deal with the world of work than British novels. This is in fact their great strength. Even a mediocre novel which places its emphasis upon work rather than leisure has at least a documentary interest.

You can, of course, write a superb novel which doesn't concern itself with work at all and which has a limited number of settings or even only one setting. None of your characters need have a job. If they do have jobs, they can pass the time when doing them in a waking dream. And it's true that for the majority of people work at best is bearable, and their real life begins when they go home.

But this book's function is to instruct you how to write a novel which will be published. And the best way of doing this is to devote at least a third of your space to your characters at work and to vary your settings as much as is credible. If you use the same one twice, there should be a good reason for it. Don't think of a situation, then hunt round for a setting; think of situation and setting together.

One setting you should be careful about is the bedroom. It isn't so much that your characters should make love in other places as that there is more to sex than the act itself. It isn't, for most of us, something which we switch on inside the bedroom and switch off out of it. It pervades our whole waking lives—and our dreams too—and can affect actions which are apparently quite unrelated to it. You don't have to study psychology in order to know about it—you have only to observe other people and to be quite honest with yourself.

What should be avoided is too explicit a description of the sexual act itself. For, providing that it's actually completed, this is much the same for everybody, unless they're double-jointed and extremely inventive. What isn't the same is the people and the circumstances, their thoughts and their actual physical surroundings. And, irrespective of personal beliefs and morals, every time a sexual act takes place between two human beings a relation is formed which is essentially non-physical, which lasts beyond the act. I don't know whether this is purely a Western phenomenon, the consequence of two thousand years of the Christian tradition. I don't, speaking as a novelist, particularly care. What concerns me is that the relationship exists. Its existence isn't, needless to say, conveyed by abstract statements, but by concrete description of the feelings and actions of the people concerned.

I'm diffident about saying this, but I believe that if you can't

see sex with a certain wonder it's better not to write about it at
all. To be honest with yourself about it means that you must
acknowledge its power to change your life, to bring to it a kind
of wildness, to transform the commonplace. You need have
no illusions about the object of your desire or about the
ultimate end of your relationship, but what you feel is much
more than tumescence.

While we were at dinner heavy snow was descending
outside. This downfall had ceased by the time my things
were collected, though a few flakes were still blowing about
in the clear winter air when we set out at last for the
Templers' house. The wind had suddenly dropped. The
night was very cold.

"Had to sell the Buick," Templer said. "I'm afraid you
won't find much room at the back of this miserable
vehicle."

Mona, now comatose after the wine at dinner, rolled
herself up in a rug and took the seat in front. Almost
immediately she went to sleep. Jean and I sat at the back of
the car. We passed through Hammersmith, and the
neighbourhood of Chiswick: then out on to the Great West
Road. For a time I made desultory conversation. At last she
scarcely answered and I gave it up. Templer, smoking a
cigar in the front, also seemed disinclined to talk now that
he was at the wheel. We drove along at a good rate.

On either side of the highway, grotesque buildings, which
in daytime resembled the temples of some shoddy, utterly
unsympathetic Atlantis, now assumed the appearance of an
Arctic city's frontier forts. Veiled in snow, these hideous
monuments of a lost world bordered a broad river of black,
foaming slush, across the surface of which the car skimmed
and jolted with a harsh crackling sound, as if the liquid
beneath were scalding hot.

Although not always simultaneous in taking effect, nor

necessarily at all equal in voltage, the process of love is rarely unilateral. When the moment comes, a secret attachment is often returned with interest. Some know this by instinct; others learn in a hard school.

The exact spot must have been a few hundred yards beyond the point where the electrically illuminated young lady in a bathing dress dives eternally through the petrol-tainted air; night and day, winter and summer, never reaching the water of the pool to which she endlessly glides. Like some image of arrested development, she returns for ever, voluntarily, to the springboard from which she started her leap. A few seconds after I had seen this bathing belle journeying, as usual, imperturbably through the frozen air, I took Jean in my arms.

Her response, so sudden and passionate, seemed surprising only a minute or two later. All at once everything was changed. Her body felt at the same time hard and yielding, giving a kind of glow as if live current issued from it. I used to wonder afterwards whether, in the last resort, of all the time we spent together, however ecstatic, those first moments on the Great West Road were not the best.[35]

This extract from Anthony Powell's *The Acceptance World* is the model of how it should be done. When the narrator takes Jean in his arms, it's almost superfluous. It's the snow and the cold and the sound of the car tires on the slush which tell us what's going to happen; existence is transformed. The narrator doesn't say that it's transformed; he sets everything down as he saw it. What is important, after the embrace, is the thought that this was the best time of all—which is quiet, true, and implicitly sad.

What follows eventually is a hasty dialogue:

"Where shall I find you?"
"Next to you on the left."
"How soon?"

"Give it half an hour."
"I'll be there."
"Don't be too long."
She laughed softly when she said that, disengaging
herself from the rug that covered both of us.[36]

We don't follow them into the bedroom. What follows the
next morning, is a further description of his host's house.
Nothing is described of what happened between Jean and the
narrator. The emphasis is on the other guests. The narrator
finds no opportunity to be alone with her. The day wears on:

All the while I felt horribly bored with the whole lot of
them, longing to be alone once more with Jean, and yet also
in some odd manner almost dreading the moment when that
time should come; one of those mixed sensations so
characteristic of intense emotional excitement. There is
always the element of unreality, perhaps even of slight
absurdity, about someone you love. It seemed to me that
she was sitting in an awkward, almost melodramatic
manner, half-turned towards Quiggin, while she crumbled
her bread with fingers long and subtly shaped. I seemed to
be looking at a picture of her, yet felt that I could easily lose
control of my senses, and take her, then and there, in my
arms. [37]

He finally manages to be alone with her and, almost
reluctantly, she arranged to see him again:

In spite of apparent coldness of manner her eyes were
full of tears. As if we had already decided upon some
definite and injudicious arrangement, she suddenly changed
her approach.
"You must be discreet," she said.
"All right."
"But really discreet."

John Braine

"I promise."

"You will?"

"Yes."

While talking, we had somehow come close together in a manner that made practical discussion difficult. I felt tired and rather angry, and very much in love with her; on the edge of one of those outbursts of irritation so easily excited by love.

"I'll come to your flat on Friday," she said abruptly. [38]

Somehow or other, never explicitly, we've been told about everything which happened between them. We experience the reality of their passion, and also are given foreknowledge of its unhappy end. Jean's the wrong woman for him, but he doesn't care.

But as the supreme and classic example of how to be erotic in the proper sense of the word there is his visit to Jean's flat:

Still thinking of such things, I rang the bell of the ground-floor flat. It was in an old-fashioned red-brick block of buildings, situated somewhere beyond Rutland Gate, concealed among obscure turnings that seemed to lead nowhere. For some time there was no answer to the ring. I waited, peering through the frosted glass of the front door, feeling every second an eternity. Then the door opened a few inches and Jean looked out. I saw her face only for a moment. She was laughing.

"Come in," she said quickly. "It's cold."

As I entered the hall, closing the door behind me, she ran back along the passage. I saw that she wore nothing but a pair of slippers.[39]

There follows only a brief description of the interior of the flat and a brief dialogue, which doesn't use any four-letter words. There is no description of Jean's body or of the sexual act itself, beyond that "there was no sound except her sharp intake of breath."[40]

136

This is exactly what I meant when, earlier in the book, I referred to the way in which a most laconic description can become charged with meaning from all that has preceded it. No physical detail could have added anything to this passage. With sex in particular it's more important to know what sort of people are making love than to know how they make love.

Another way of dealing with sex is through metaphor, the notorious example of which is the earth moving for Robert Jordan and Maria in *For Whom the Bell Tolls*. A straightforward physical description, even at the risk of being pornographic, would be preferable. The great objection to metaphor about sex is that one doesn't always know what is happening. It becomes even more confusing if tricks are played with punctuation and spacing and an attempt is made at a stream-of-consciousness style.

If metaphor is used, the imagery must be firmly based in reality. If it describes the sensations of one of the participants, it must be of the kind which would naturally occur to them. Four-letter words should be avoided. As a general rule, the conversation of the people involved shouldn't use sexual terms even when something sexual is being referred to. It shouldn't be forgotten, either, that sex can be funny:

"Who is he?" The floor of the bedroom was strewn with clothes—underwear, dresses, skirts, blouses, in neat piles or untidy heaps. The two wardrobes, the dressing-table and the chest-of-drawers were in matching white and gilt, with glass tops. The brushes and hand mirror on the dressing-table were gold-backed, and there was scarcely room for all the bottles of perfume and powder and hand lotion and hair-spray and, lonely in its brown utility, a large bottle of Milton. There was a white-painted bookcase full of new books; at least a dozen of these had found their way on to the floor.

"He's very rich," she said. "Do you know, I've never

found a rich man who wasn't at bottom terribly sweet? But he can be *so* gloomy. He takes all kinds of pills, and he's always going on special diets. His name's Amroth, actually. He has a terrible inferiority complex because he isn't quite a millionaire. So his brother's going to make him a millionaire.''

"That's nice."

"Yes, it is. Because though his brother's a millionaire, he doesn't really agree with him. About politics, I mean. His brother's Left, like that sweet old Mislingford, and R.A.'s very right-wing. I'm sure you'd like him."

"You must introduce me."

"Oh, I'm sure you'd get on together famously. R.A.'s very clever. He worries a lot about the country."

"So do I." I allowed myself to indulge in a political fantasy. The details weren't quite clear, but always resolved themselves in a cheering mob carrying me shoulder-high to Buckingham Palace. My eyes began to close.

"Do you want a drink?"

"A little one."

She jumped out of bed and into a pair of black high-heeled shoes; as I watched her naked figure, slim but not with the skinniness of the professional model, disappear, I breathed in the smell of the bedroom—tobacco, scent, clean linen, sex—in a haze of contentment. I moved over to her side of the bed and felt the warmth of her imprint, stretching on it like a cat. There would be no talk of shame, no need to tell lies about love. That would be the attraction for Amroth, who presumably would have paid for it all. That—and as I remembered now, he was in his late forties—the ego-enhancing pleasure of being seen with her. And her untidiness, her vast frivolous carelessness, would be another attraction; here he could, so to speak, let down his hair. Everything was permissible in this bedroom.

She reappeared with a bottle of Black and White and two glasses on a tray. We sat up in bed drinking and talking or rather she talked and I listened. It was a flow of soothing prattle—she lay in bed until noon, she shopped mainly at Harrods, she used to hunt, but she couldn't bear what happened to the poor fox, she loved to eat but not sweet things any more, she was pestering R.A. to buy her a Mini and she was going to have a psychedelic paint job done on it—she lived by her body, for her body, through her body, completely adjusted to the world of the senses, stroking each moment with whimpers of delight like a new mink coat.

Then she stopped and smiled. "I believe there's a hubbub in the plaza, darling. Yes there is, there truly is. . . ."

I almost screamed as the soft apparently boneless hand touched me.

"Oh Christ. Wonderful. Wonderful."

"We can't let it go to waste. Can we? Can we? Can we?" Her voice was rising higher and higher.[41]

I could, of course, have found a far more explicit way of putting the girl's remark about the hubbub in the plaza, but it wouldn't have added anything to the story. And, to my mind at least, it wouldn't have been as erotic. The use of the rather fancy, lighthearted metaphor is—or at least I intended it to be—another aspect of the girl's sensuousness; it overflows into language, but not into sexual language. The sensuousness is that proper to its medium.

Most of what I have said about sex applies to violence. This is obviously essential to the thriller. The morality of writing about it at all isn't my province. But whether you're writing a thriller or a straight novel, you should never tell lies about it and you should always be accurate about it. Violence is part of life, but not necessarily part of everyone's life. I myself have managed to survive for over fifty years so far without seeing very much of it. It doesn't figure very much in my novels precisely because of this. It doesn't have to figure in your novel. The less there is of it, the more shock value it has when it appears.

The "death car," as the newspapers called it, didn't stop; it came out of the gathering darkness, wavered tragically for a moment, and then disappeared around the next bend. Mavromichaelis wasn't even sure of its colour—he told the first policeman that it was light green. The other car, the one going towards New York, came to rest a hundred yards beyond, and its driver hurried back to where Myrtle Wilson, her life violently extinguished, knelt in the road and mingled her thick dark blood with the dust.

Michaelis and this man reached her first, but when they had torn open her shirtwaist, still damp with perspiration, they saw that her left breast was swinging loose like a flap, and there was no need to listen for the heart beneath. The mouth was wide open and ripped a little at the corners, as though she had choked a little in giving up the tremendous vitality she had stored so long.[42]

The consequence of this death is two more deaths:

The chauffeur—he was one of Wolfsheim's protégés—heard the shots—afterwards he could only say that he hadn't thought anything much about them. I drove from the station directly to Gatsby's house and my rushing anxiously up the front steps was the first thing that alarmed anyone. But they knew then, I firmly believe. With scarcely a word said, four of us, the chauffeur, butler, gardener, and I, hurried down to the pool.

There was a faint, barely perceptible movement of the water as the fresh flow from one end urged its way towards the drain at the other. With little ripples that were hardly the shadows of waves, the laden mattress moved irregularly down the pool. A small gust of wind that scarcely corrugated the surface was enough to disturb its accidental course with its accidental burden. The touch of a cluster of leaves revolved it slowly, tracing, like the leg of transit, a thin red circle in the water.

It was after we started with Gatsby towards the house that the gardener saw Wilson's body a little way off in the grass, and the holocaust was complete.[43]

And that's the sum total of the violence in *The Great Gatsby*. It's described accurately, almost clinically—the narrator sees the three deaths with all the clarity of shock. Three human beings have died. There isn't any need for him to dwell on it, to say how dreadful it is. The horror and the pity are all implicit. There is, too, something more to Gatsby's death; quiet-spoken and amiable though he is, he's a professional bootlegger, and part of a world of violence. Violence has caught up with him.

I end with a contradictory statement. It is quite possible to write a good novel—completely unsentimental and truthful—in which there is no sex and no violence and no real suffering of any kind. There are people who manage to go through life without encountering any of these realities. They manage to close their eyes to anything which they don't want to see. They have a perfect right to, and it isn't the novelist's job to judge them. People like this are perfectly legitimate subjects for the novelist. The novelist doesn't have to present the whole of life, only that part of life which he knows about and can handle. But if you write such a novel, then somehow there must be in it the consciousness of a world existing where there is sex and violence and suffering. Whether your characters think about the whole of reality or not, you are bound to. You have also to bear in mind that to lead a sheltered life is only possible because there are people who don't lead sheltered lives. I don't know how you convey the existence of what we'll call the real world, except, again, by telling the truth. One part of the truth will always reveal the whole.

NINE: The quick and the dead

And yet there are people writing first novels now who will break most, if not all, of my rules. Their novels will be accepted and their novels will be good novels. They may even be better novels than mine. They may also be enormously successful. The last and the most important rule of all is that there aren't any rules.

Put it this way: You can be directly autobiographical, you can make propaganda, you can move dizzily backwards and forwards in time, you can be wrong about idiom, you can tack description on to each character like a cheap ready-made suit, you can wander in and out of the narrative making long involved statements about abstract ideas, you can write execrable prose, you can write an absurdly short novel or an absurdly long novel, you can even be experimental. You don't have to describe your characters at all—O'Hara didn't. (And in his first—some assert his best—novel he tells the story from the viewpoint of more than one character, precisely the method I don't recommend.) You may even, like Thomas Wolfe, write at such length and so repetitiously that the publisher has to reshape it.

There isn't a fault I've named that you can't get away with. And though I believe that the method of working which I've proposed is the best, it isn't the only one. You can make up the novel as you go along, you can work only when you feel like it or under the influence of alcohol or whatever your favourite drug may be. You may write version after version until you've got it right. You may ask—and take—advice from others or you may prefer not to talk about your work with anybody. You may write for writing's sake or you may write just for the money. And, of course, you may write your first novel long before the age which I recommend.

No one can tell you which rules to break and when—whether my rules or anybody else's. But whatever I've written about the novel has had one purpose behind it: To make it easier for someone to write the only kind of novel I care about.

I have already quoted from the novels which have the quality towards which I have aimed since my first novel; when I add them to those on the list at the end of the book, there aren't very many. Mostly as a reader one has to settle for rather less, for novels which have only a modicum of what one hankers for, or, as in the case of some thrillers, offer one a reasonably palatable substitute, custard cream instead of dairy cream. The truth is always in conflict with the demands of the literature industry—departments of English, publishers and journalists, who must find something to write and talk about and learn about and earn dividends from and who really do award A's for Effort.

But real writing isn't like that at all, any more than a battle is like a game of chess. Granted that the literature industry now, being Leftwards inclined, values—or says it values —popular culture and whatever is unfeigned and spontaneous and preferably by the underprivileged and non-white, it still lives by abstract theory. As long as this abstract theory is what counts, then anyone who has the kind of intelligence to master it can be, if there is any justice in the scheme of things, creative too. Tied up with this is the notion of the writer's wholehearted dedication—achieved only by being in constant spiritual training, an academic Galahad. Galahad lives by a fixed set of moral principles, maturing at a measurable rate, and each novel contributes to his achievement—which is a true awareness of himself and the universe.

John Braine

And all that has as much to do with creative writing as a graph in a sex survey has to do with actually making love. It isn't that a great deal can't be learned from some members of the literature industry; there still exists a handful of genuine interpreters and discoverers, who know and love and serve literature. But what counts for the novelist—and for every creative writer—is knowing when to cast the rules aside, knowing when they are merely a constriction of that vitality you must drive towards.

It is that which means readability, like that quality in a few actors which makes you watch everything they do or say, no matter how commonplace. Looking back, I haven't described the quality very well; perhaps I daren't, and perhaps it isn't healthy for a creative writer to think too much about these matters. I always have in my mind the story of W. C. Fields in his juggling days, reading Hazlitt on juggling and discovering how clever he was, how a juggler could slice a second up into a hundred different and distinct parts, how miraculous his coordination was, how the essence of juggling was a dance on the edge of disaster, or words to that effect. He read this with fascination and a growing sense of wonder; the next time he went on stage he dropped everything.

But it's essential that you should understand what it is that you're trying to do, how important it is to keep the rules and how important it is to break them. So I end with the only statement about the nature and the function of the novel which I've ever been able to read without irritation. D. H. Lawrence was a flawed novelist, but a great writer, and here, definitively, he thinks the matter through:

> You can fool pretty nearly every other medium. You can make a poem pietistic, and still it will be a poem. You can write *Hamlet* in drama: if you wrote him in a novel, he'd be half comic, or a trifle suspicious: a suspicious character, like Dostoyevsky's Idiot. Somehow, you sweep the ground

144

a bit too clear in the poem or the drama, and you let the human Word fly a bit too freely. Now in a novel there's always a tom-cat, a black tom-cat that pounces on the white dove of the Word, if the dove doesn't watch it; and there is a banana-skin to trip on; and you know there is a water-closet on the premises. All these things help to keep the balance. . . .

We have to choose between the quick and the dead. The quick is God-flame, in everything. And the dead is dead. In this room where I write, there is a little table that is dead: it doesn't even weakly exist. And there is a ridiculous little iron stove, which for some unknown reason is quick. And there is an iron wardrobe trunk, which for some still more mysterious reason is quick. And there are several books, whose mere corpus is dead, utterly dead and non-existent. And there is a sleeping cat, very quick. And a glass lamp, alas, is dead.

What makes the difference? *Quien sabe!* But difference there is. And I *know it.*

And if one tries to find out wherein the quickness of the quick lies, it is in a certain weird relationship between that which is quick and—I don't know; perhaps all the rest of the things. It seems to consist in an odd sort of fluid, changing, grotesque or beautiful relatedness. That silly iron stove somehow *belongs.* Whereas this thin-shanked table doesn't belong. It is a mere disconnected lump, like a cut-off finger.

And now we see the great, great merits of the novel. It can't exist without being "quick". The ordinary unquick novel, even if it be a best seller, disappears into absolute nothingness, the dead burying their dead with surprising speed. For even the dead like to be tickled. But the next minute, they've forgotten both the tickling and the tickler.

Secondly, the novel contains no didactic absolute. All that is quick, and all that is said and done by the quick, is in

145

some way godly. So that Vronsky's taking Anna Karenina we must count godly, since it is quick. And that Prince in *Resurrection*, following the convict girl, we must count dead. The convict train is quick and alive. But that would-be-expiatory Prince is as dead as lumber.

The novel itself lays down these laws for us, and we spend our time evading them. The man in the novel must be "quick". And this means one thing, among a host of unknown meaning: it means he must have a quick relatedness to all the other things in the novel: snow, beg-bugs, sunshine, the phallus, trains, silk-hats, cats, sorrow, people, food, diphtheria, fuchsias, stars, ideas, God, tooth-paste, lightning, and toilet-paper. He must be in quick relation to all these things. What he says and does must be relative to them all.[44]

That, regardless of genre, is the only kind of novel which matters—the quick, the alive. If this book helps in the writing of only one such novel, it will have succeeded in its purpose.

TEN: The quick

What follows isn't an exhaustive bibliography but a brief list of books—novels and non-fiction—which you should have read before you begin to write your novel. Either they demonstrate in practice how a novel should be written or, if non-fiction, have something useful to say about the novel and writing in general. I don't mean that you don't need any others. Any book that you read with pleasure has something to teach you, if only how to keep a story moving.

There is no book on this list which I have not read with pleasure, nor which I shall not read again with pleasure. I did not read them in the first place to improve my prose and narrative technique or increase my understanding of human nature. You'll notice that with the exception of the Dostoyevsky and the Thomas Mann, none of them yet is a classic, its status indisputable. The great novels you should have read anyway. The bulk of your reading must now be contemporary: a good writer belongs to his time, lives in the present. Because he does this, in a strange way his work keeps its freshness, doesn't go musty.

AMIS, KINGSLEY: *Lucky Jim*
The main reason for the success of this novel—and for the fact that it's still in print—is quite simply that it's funny. It was meant to be funny. It wasn't written in order to change the world; it isn't a blistering satire. Jim Dixon, the hero, is mildly Left Wing, but the only person he's interested in doing

147

good to is himself. In the end, against all expectations, he snatches not only his rival's girlfriend from under his nose, but also the marvellous job in London of which his rival feels assured. What is more, he gloats over his rival's humiliation; he isn't a gentleman. The background is a provincial university; the originality here is that the author completely departs from the Oxbridge tradition of dreaming spires and port-bibbing wise old dons, and shows the place as it is. Contrary to the notion put about by literary journalists, there were few novelists following Amis who used this background. And if there have been any comic novels since with the same dazzling display of high spirits, I haven't heard of them.

COLETTE: *Chéri* and *The Last of Chéri*

These two books tell the story of a love affair between a young man and a very much older woman—a *grande cocotte* who has taken care of her figure and finances. In the end, without meaning to, she destroys her lover's marriage and destroys him. For what he has had from her he can never have from any other woman; he has had—not in any narrow moral sense—more than he should have had, and he's forced to pay for it.

Colette's domain is the world of the senses; no writer has ever re-created it so longingly, so unremittingly, and so remorselessly. To read this novel—for the two books must be regarded as an entity—is almost a physical experience. I shouldn't have to add this: By "the world of the senses" I don't only mean sexuality. She writes about a dress, a meal, a flower, a piece of furniture with the same precise and enraptured sensuality as she does about the act of love. Most novelists, compared with her, seem to inhabit a sparse bare world where the only physical pleasure is sex. I can think of no other novelist from whom you can learn so much.

COOPER, WILLIAM: *Scenes from Provincial Life*

Despite the impression given by the conventional literary

histories—the Age of Classicism, the Age of Romanticism, the Age of Realism, and so on—there isn't any given moment at which all writers begin writing in a new way, any more than in our homes there is a given moment when we throw out all our old furniture and install new. Yet the way in which we write does change, and somehow or other the old furniture disappears. There are seminal books, originators, after which nothing is the same again. Sometimes they may be copied, almost plagiarized, but what most often happens is that they're learned from. I and others learned a good deal from *Scenes from Provincial Life:* most of all to relax, to keep it cool, to talk rather than write, to go right up to the reader rather than keep our distance as conscious artists. There was something else too; high spirits and enjoyment and not giving a damn about the state of the world. It's about private people; and if ever I'd been tempted towards the novel of commitment, I put the thought aside after reading William Cooper. And yet I recommend it to you for none of these reasons, but simply because it's an exceptionally skilful novel which has never had its fair share of notice—largely, I suspect, since Cooper has never made the requisite amount of solemn pronouncement about the Human Condition.

DOSTOYEVSKY, FEDOR: *The Brothers Karamazov*
You won't learn anything from this novel about literary technique. I wouldn't suggest that you should take him as your model. If there are any rules, mine or anyone else's, of the novel, he breaks them all. And this is absolutely irrelevant because there has never been a greater novel, one which goes so deeply into human life and its purpose. In comparison, novels by other writers are full of lies—well-intentioned lies, beautifully reasoned lies, but lies just the same. And there hasn't been another novel which is so fiercely and outrageously alive, the ultimate justification of the form. It's Dostoyevsky's last book, into which he put his whole experience and all his genius. When you have read it, you'll be no better

John Braine

equipped to write your own novel; but if you haven't read it, you'll have diminished yourself as a human being and as a writer.

Dos Passos, John: *U.S.A. (The 42nd Parallel, Nineteen Nineteen, The Big Money)*

If at times in this book I've seemed to have very little respect for present-day critics, the neglect of John Dos Passos is one of the reasons. This is a novel in three volumes rather than a trilogy and should be read as a whole. It's over one thousand pages in the paperback edition and spans the period from the turn of the century to the beginning of the Depression. It's episodic in treatment, and the stories of the main characters are interposed with *Newsweek*—snatches of popular songs—extracts from newspapers, Camera Eye passages—streams-of-consciousness unconnected with the main characters—and potted biographies. The lives of the main characters interact with each other. It is very consciously a novel of social realism, and the intention is to give a picture of the life of a nation. The U.S.A. is the hero, and the characters are meant to be regarded as aspects of the U.S.A. I add to this that its bias is Left Wing, and its ending—the vagrant trying to thumb a lift: to where, he doesn't know—is quite specifically the kind of ending I don't recommend. But it succeeds: We're given a picture of the whole of American life; this is authentically the Great American Novel. His characters aren't the mouthpieces for his political ideas, but living human beings. I don't know whether anyone else could make the documentary technique work like Dos Passos or to what extent he could be one of the great teachers, like Joyce. I am sure that he is, of all twentieth-century novelists, the most unjustly neglected.

Greene, Graham: *The End of the Affair*

The main drawback of the first-person narrative is

150

eliminated here by making the narrator a professional novelist. It is my favourite among Greene's novels because its English background, to me at least, makes it more immediate and convincing. Quite illogically, I feel with an exotic background anything may happen; the unlikely loses much of its shock value. I cannot always accept his themes; they seem too contrived, too much at variance with the realities of human nature as I know them. But I can accept the main theme of this novel, which is that grace can descend upon the most unlikely people, that you don't qualify for it by good behaviour and the correct beliefs, that God moves in a mysterious and arbitrary way. The ending comes with an unexpected force, a sad haunted tenderness—love against the grain, God forcing His gift on a recipient who, like it or not, must use it.

GROSSMITH, GEORGE and WEEDON: *The Diary of a Nobody*

I specifically don't include this as an example of how a novel should be written because that implies that you could learn from the authors' technique and their viewpoint of their subject, that you could continue in the same direction. It isn't possible: This is a one-off job. I don't believe that the Grossmith brothers gave any thought to technique; they simply presented Mr. Porter, the city clerk, exactly as he saw himself.

Mr. Porter is one of God's holy innocents. He sees no evil in anyone else because there is no evil in himself. He has no envy; he accepts in their entirety the standards of his time and environment. Without any sociological or satirical or political purpose, the life of a typical member of the lower-middle classes in Holloway in 1891 is permanently preserved. It's gently, subtly comic—Mr. Porter is a born victim—but comic with love, written with love.

But "written" is the wrong word. George Grossmith was an actor, Weedon an entertainer. They weren't really novelists at

John Braine

all, but men of the theatre. I can't imagine that the book was
planned or revised; it's miraculously spontaneous. I don't
think that they chose to write it: It is as if it had already been
written, or rather, been created, and it had chosen them.

KARP, DAVID: *One*

This is a novel of the future which doesn't specify the date
or give any clues like references to the Third World War or
new forms of transport or ways of dress or speech. It isn't
science fiction. You're aware that you're in the future without
being told so. Being told so is precisely what makes novels
about the future unreal, for no one in the future is conscious
of living in the future. And what will be significant about the
future won't be its material changes, but the changes in the
philosophy and purpose of government. This novel was
published in 1954, and since then everything that has been
happening in the West—particularly in education—has
contributed to its enormous prophetic force. This is not a
propaganda novel. It deals with the conflict between the
traditional concept of the sacredness of the individual and the
new concept of absolute equality. It isn't to be thought of as
anti-Communist or even anti-Socialist. It goes far beyond that
and it is far more frightening and credible and, in the end,
without flourish or melodrama, far more genuinely hopeful.
The hero, who from first to last accepts the philosophy of
equality, is defeated, as the Jews were defeated at the Rising
of the Warsaw Ghetto. But, when you think about them, they
were not defeated.

MANN, THOMAS: *Death in Venice*

If you're impelled to write a short novel, then technically
this must be your model. It isn't an extended short story or a
condensed novel; it is a short novel of exactly the right length.
Nothing has been left out which bears on the theme; it is
completely and totally satisfying. The picture of age and

achievement, dedication and descipline, suddenly crumbling into decadence, a senile shameless obsession, is absolutely complete. It isn't only physical beauty which conquers the hero, but Venice with its atmosphere of everything being permitted. The hero crumbles with a terrifying speed into a painted grotesque, the discipline of a lifetime abandoned, all restraint and dignity thrown away. But the flaw isn't made by Venice, but discovered by Venice; it was there all the time. Perhaps no novel as perfect as this will ever be written again; but unless you read it, you can't even begin to try to emulate it.

SMITH, STEVIE: *Novel on Yellow Paper*

Stevie Smith wasn't really a novelist at all, but a poet, and this novel isn't really a novel. Of course it's autobiographical: Stevie Smith is speaking directly to us, whatever she may call herself in the narrative. Whether any of it happened or not is beside the point. And nothing very spectacular does happen, except the most spectacular and rare event of all—a human voice speaking with utter frankness. Feminine, quirky, sardonic, knowledgeable about love and even more about death, possessed of an enormous angular, slightly spinsterish vitality, there has never been anyone quite like the owner of this voice, never a prose so dry, swift, helter-skelter, and breathlessly individual. This is what can be done with the first-person singular; it could be done only once, but she didn't care about that; in her vocabulary "career" and "success" had no place.

SOLZHENITSYN, ALEXANDER: *The First Circle*

The word "great" should never be used lightly. It should virtually never be used of books written during an author's lifetime. In the case of a brave man like Solzhenitsyn, cruelly persecuted by the Soviet authorities, his work now forbidden in the U.S.S.R., we must be doubly careful. There is no necessary connection between greatness of moral stature and greatness of suffering and literary greatness. It is a good beginning to have a great theme—in this instance the nature of freedom—but no more than a beginning. As I've said elsewhere, literary talent, like grace, doesn't always fall upon those who deserve it. One must take into account, too, that this book can be—indeed has been—used as a weapon in the Cold War. It wasn't written for that purpose, though since it tells the truth about the society the author lived in, it is bound to reveal that that society is a tyranny. It was written to reveal the limits of tyranny; in the end the prisoners being transported to a new prison, a lower circle of Hell, are more free than the people outside, for they have nothing more to lose. There is no hope offered in this book, only the fact that there is a last freedom which is indestructible. It must be read because only now can we hear the author at maximum intensity, receive his whole message. The language changes, ways of living change; in a hundred years from now this will still be read, it will be confirmed in its greatness. But already there will be a little dust to obscure our vision; it will be a handful of scholars who get the most from it.

TRILLING, LIONEL: *The Middle of the Journey*

The traditional jeer at critics is that they're like eunuchs; they know how to do it but can't. This novel is in a way a miracle. It isn't possible on the face of it for anyone who is so completely dedicated a critic, who knows so much about the art of the novel, to produce a novel which is without any doubt quick in D. H. Lawrence's sense, live, not an illustration of a theme, but a story about a human being and the change in his whole way of living which is brought about by involvement with other human beings. Furthermore, the main characters are intellectuals; their concern is with the world of ideas. The moving force of the novel is the arrival of Gifford Maxim, who has—this is necessarily an oversim-

plification—rejected Communism for religion. Again—and
it's essential you should understand this—this is not an
anti-Communist novel. A good novel isn't anti-anything or
pro-anything either. As much as anything, this novel is about
love. In one sense, because it's so superbly planned, so
faithful in its details, so solid in texture without one
superfluous word, it's very easy to read. In another
sense—and here he has something in common with Dostoyevsky—it's terribly hard to read. There are some
happenings which, when presented truthfully, are too much to
bear. And there is a quality of a few beings which almost hurts
with its brightness—the ability to love, simplicity of heart.
The ability to recognize this quality, much less to project it,
isn't encountered very often in contemporary novels. It's
reason enough to read and study this novel.

I recommend no books on the technique of the novel since
it's better that you make a list for yourself or ask your local
librarian to make up one for you. (It's part of his job, and he'll
be delighted to do it.) But do not on any account fail to read
Cyril Connolly's *Enemies of Promise.* It isn't a manual of
technique. It's in two parts. The first is a wonderfully concise
record of the author's youth, the second a consideration of
the creative process and the pitfalls which beset the writer.
Above all, and with an authority which hasn't been matched
before or since, what makes good prose—to quote Hemingway again, the kind which doesn't go bad—is defined with a
clarity which will rid you of all your illusions. This is the book
which taught a whole generation to write; and if it doesn't
teach another generation, it will only be because we've
allowed it to be forgotten. If Connolly had written nothing
else, this would be enough.

ELEVEN: The history of my own first novel

Early in 1951 I resigned my job at Bingley Public Library in Yorkshire to become a free-lance writer in London. It's easy now to say that it was the most sensible decision of my whole life, that if I hadn't taken it I should now be simply a provincial librarian, and a frustrated one at that. It was also the cause, within less than a year, of a breakdown in health that took two years to be put right.

I don't recommend anyone to do what I did. In 1939 it was possible for anyone with even a modicum of literary ability to earn a subsistence in London or in New York; there were many more publications, and cheap accommodation near the centre was easily available. By 1951 the number of publications had drastically shrunk, payment for contributions was far behind the increase in the cost of living, and there wasn't any cheap accommodation. And, of course, the situation is even worse today. To leave home for the capital—or simply to leave home—is essential for most writers because they need not only personal freedom but a distance between themselves and their material. But they should get a decent job first.

In July my present agent, David Higham, read an article of mine about my Irish grandmother in the *New Statesman* and, through Paul Scott, at that time in charge of the fiction side of Higham's, suggested that Higham's should represent me. On the strength of the *New Statesman* article, Paul Scott felt that I was capable of writing a novel. So I went away and wrote it.

But this is to make it appear too easy. I went away and thought about the novel and made odd notes about it when I wasn't trying to place articles to get the money to eat and pay the rent. I knew that I could write a novel; the one thing I didn't have was time.

It began with a picture in my mind of a man I knew who used to take a girl I knew to a disused brickworks high above the moors in Bingley. The brickworks was just off the road and he parked his car in the shelter of the kiln. The road was very little used, and it was cold and windy up there. Not very many people had cars in England at that period, particularly young ones; cars, any cars, had a glamour about them which they don't have now.

Neither the man nor the girl was married, but the girl had a close relationship with someone else which I haven't yet been able to understand. I don't want to go any further into it because already I feel uncomfortable writing about real people and because—which is more important—I want to find out more about the girl's relationship with the other person. When I do, it all can be made into another novel. The other novel will have nothing to do with my first novel.

What mattered about that man and that girl wasn't what they felt for each other or what the man was like as a person. In the picture that I had in my mind, he was in fact alone in his car by the disused brickworks just after sunset on an autumn evening. There was a girl in his mind; she'd gone away or died, she wasn't going to be with him again, but in the picture she wasn't the girl I knew any more than he was the man I knew. Only the narrow winding road and the drystone walls and the short springy grass were drawn from the life.

As I remember, I made notes during 1951, deciding fairly early that there would be a triangle, that Joe, then Joe Lambert, would marry the rich man's daughter and lose the woman he really wanted. It wasn't until I went into the hospital in 1952 that I had the time to concentrate on the

157

John Braine

novel. I was extremely ill, but I wasn't in any pain, and I didn't have to worry about earning a living. I made more notes, did what research was necessary, and began the first draft (C).

As I've already explained, this went in the wrong direction. There was far too much detail about what was irrelevant to the story; it would have been exactly what was needed if I'd been writing a novel about Joe Lampton at seventeen, but that wasn't my intention; he had in the last chapter to be in his car by the disused brickworks, and that meant a gap of at least nine years.

It was useful also to describe the countryside around Warley—significantly, including the stretch of road where Alice was to die. But there was too much of it. It got in the way of the story. And the conversation between the café proprietor and Joe was going to cause problems. If so much space was given to him, then it could only be because he had an important part to play in the story: I didn't see where he'd fit in.

The notes which follow were mostly written after I'd finished the first draft and had made the decision to write it in the first person. I had a feeling that I was very near what I wanted in the first draft; the *density* was right, some of the detail was wonderfully accurate (one has to be able to say this without conceit). But, though I didn't know the phrase then in that connection, I still hadn't found the right tone of voice. Once I decided upon first person narrative, there were no problems left except time, time to work at my own pace. And that I took care never to run out of again. I shall run out of it, as we all shall; but I shall never again waste it.

What follows, in roughly chronological order, are the actual extracts from my notes and first drafts.

158

WRITING A NOVEL

(A) NOTES--1st draft

BORN FAVOURITE

(1st TITLE)

(1)   Joe is dreaming. He's playing cricket.
Maureen is there. He awakes. Late August, Saturday morning.
He feels happy still from the dream. From his window he can
see the moors. Looks at himself in the mirror, pleased.
Goes to Town Hall. Tardoff says Maureen in yesterday. Joe
goes to Rates Office to sell some theatre tickets. Thinks of
Maureen.

(2)   Maureen at breakfast. Ackroyd talking with
her. Shopping. Morning coffee. Sees A.'s mistress. Like
Olive. Angry. Is cast for show. Thinks of this.

(3)   Reading. Introduce producer Reg. M. going
into street wind and rain thinks of Joe.

(4)   Working party. J. kisses M. How to make all
characters inter-relate?
Start with Joe that's certain. We leave him thinking of Maureen. We show where he lives, something of Throw-
ton, and something of the Town Hall. Next chapter Music
Hall: he can talk with Maureen and see Susan. But it's
Susan he's after, and Susan he thinks of when he leaves. Next
chapter goes over to M. angry with A. at morning--shopping,
coffee with casting secretary who tells her she's cast with
J. Sees A.'s mistress, isn't jealous but angry. Next we see
Joe with Susan at dance. No, this still won't do. It's the
mechanical difficulties which are the worst though--if J. has

a car, what about M.? Why, he can always give her a lift and
they can embrace in the car first of all. Always give her a
lift, that is, when he hasn't other fish to fry; or someone
else doesn't. Car no good for first embrace, though. He's
invited to her house; she tempts him there? No, the car
would do. But what precipitates it, since it hasn't happened
before? He gives her a lift after the reading, when she's
angry with A. It's early, come in for a drink. <u>Then</u> it can
happen. But this is not repeated because she feels constrained in the house. (1) Joe alone (2) Music Hall: Joe (3)
Maureen, morning and library (4) Maureen: Reading (5) Rehearsal: J. thinking of Susan. He gives M. a lift.

     Diffuculty again. I want their coming together not
to be the consequence of stage lovemaking, or to be capable
of being so construed.

     Make 4 and 5 one; interpose chapter about M. discov-
ering A. really is sleeping with Olive. (Maybe I don't like
the whole damned thing. I've got the central idea straight
and the main character and that's about all. Well, I'll write
it <u>all</u>, even if I have to rewrite the whole thing. Next
chapter rehearsal, going home--lift, then come in for drink,
etc. Then social evening with Charles. Then lovers. So far
so good. Then out with Susan. Takes her to club dances,
etc. (Warned off her?) Leave it for now, think a little.
But I'm puzzled as to whether to plan the whole or not first.
I'll try not planning it all, for I already have a vague idea
of theme, etc. I'll begin at the beginning and let the story
take me with it. I won't begin another chapter until one is

properly completed--then I can see the background, the people will come alive, memories and ideas and dialogue will be real- ised. Definitely this is the best way.

John Braine

NOTES--1st draft

LAST CHAPTER

Doesn't sleep with Mrs. T. in sense of making love
to her. Is reminded of when as boy of thirteen, he went to
his mother's bed with earache--it is, he realises, like that.
Goes into her room on bare feet as if to make himself suffer.

Before--learns in morning, pleads illness about noon
--goes to George, who tells him re pregnancy. Goes on his
motor-bike comb. round--it's where they used to make love--
going very fast. Goes to Blackersford, leaves comb. gets
drunk at lunch--wanders round in park, starts drinking again--
phones Mrs. T. not coming home till late?--gets home. leaves
comb. just doesn't bother. More drink, it still has no effect.
Tells her all. Come to my room. He goes. As written...etc.
Must make it clear no copulation.

Chapter 2--3

Dreffield--work in description. Remember...Parents'
death--work in after Dreffield description when someone mentions
them again.

War Damages Commission--60% house and effects. Paid
from '48. Joe would have £1000 to come plus life insurance--
about 2/3 policy value. Say he got 2/3 of £600--about £400 in
'43--in '46 on his demob actually, and he'd have demob leave &
pay & 2 years accumulated pay from POW camp. He'd have at
least £700 in '47 when he comes to Warley; being an economical
type, he just thinks of it as a reserve & lives well within
his income, which is APT II

162

WRITING A NOVEL

Exams: <u>Institute of Municipal Treasurers &</u>
<u>Accountants</u> (F.I.M.T.A. A.I.M.T.A.) School Cert = prelim.

Inter--20 yrs. old min. 4 yrs. qualifying service

Finals--22 " " " 6 " " "

 Part 1

 Part 2

War concessions--serving or home serve. 3 yrs. war service--
Inter after 2 yrs. qualifying service. 3 yrs. war service
got Inter, may take Final Part 1 after 3 yrs. qualifying
service

and Part 2 after 4 yrs. qualifying service

∴ got Inter in POW camp in 12.44, Final Part1, 6.46, Part 2,
6.46

       Returned T.H. 1.45

       3 yrs. qual. T.H. Service then--Final Part 1, 6.46 or 6.46

       Final Part 1   Joe's age--is 1922

       _____ born. RAF, 19._____

       Cost & Works Accountants

       Excused prelim.-- Inter & Final

          Inter Part 1   exams--June & December, London...

                       B'ham...Leeds & Leicester, Liverpool,

                       Manchester, Middlesboro, Newcastle,

                       Nottingham, Sheffield

          Part 2

       Factory Organisation, Equipment, <u>Production</u>, methods

Costing (4 papers):

 Labour:

 Material:

 General Expenses:

John Braine

Methods of Costing:

<u>Final</u>

Factory Orgn, Equipment & Prodn methods

Advanced Accounting:

Law of Master & Servant

Costing (3 papers)

Municipal Treasurer's Inst.

Inter--

Accountancy

Auditing

Costing

Law

Local Govt. Finance

Rating

Final

Part 1--

Banking & Public Finance

Economics

Law

Statistics

Final--Part 2

Accountancy

Auditing

Costing

E...

Local Govt. Finance

<u>Susan</u>--Goes away to Paris & goes for holiday on Norfolk Broads with students, etc. Joe very very angry envious hates guts of rich students, etc.

WRITING A NOVEL

stet

Joe Bennett was seventeen then and had a ~~Sun~~ sports
~~byeyele~~
bicycle with chromium ~~Russ~~ forks (the kind which are upright

and bent forward about three inches at right angles). The red

paint was as bright as when he bought it in 1937 and the handle-
three
bars were unscratched. He had had a dynamo and a ~~two~~-speed

gear fitted, and in the saddlebag were ~~sandwiches~~ a packet of

ham sandwiches, a map of West Yorkshire, a quarter-pound block

of Milk Motoring, a copy of <u>Cycling</u>, and a paper-backed ~~leslie~~

novel by Leslie Charteris, and his tool-kit and ~~& and~~ black
turtle-
~~pole~~-necked sweater in case he felt cold. He was wearing a

navy-blue rayon shirt with short sleeves, fastened at the front

by a white cord, navy-blue corduroy shorts, ~~and-ankle~~ black
polo
ankle-socks, and black cycling-shoes. He had a white ~~cycling~~-

cap ~~with-a-long-neb~~ and a pair of rubber-edged goggles. His

cape, fastened to the saddlebag by a pair of straps, was still

sticky with newness. On his left wrist he had a Service Des-

patch Rider wrist-watch. It was very big with a tick like an
depressing
alarm clock; the hands were set by ~~pushing-down~~ a stem beside

the winder instead of simply lifting up the winder. He had

been given this by his friend Charles Hopkins, and the face

was yellow with age. Joe was very fond of it, however: it

was a masculine watch, the kind that a despatch rider certainly

would wear--the setting-stem had about it a suggestion of war

and steel helmets, of synchronising for zero-hour, as had the

twenty-four hour dial with the Arabic figures from 13 to 24

above the Roman. The watch and compass both had the broad kind

of strap called wrist supporters; but Joe wore them more for appearance than because his wrists needed supporting.

He had set out from his home in Dreffield at ten o'clock that morning and had driven himself rather too hard. He had come some fifty miles without stopping for food; at that time he made a cult of T. E. Lawrence, and he had just learned this was the sort of thing he used to do in order to develop that ~~Lawrence-in-his-youth-used-to-take-long-cycle-rides-with~~ his physical endurance. ~~no-food-or-with-irregular-amounts-at-irregular-intervals-in order-to-develop-his-physical-endurance.~~ His intention had been been not to eat at all; but ~~As~~ as he came into Warley he began to feel dizzy with hunger. He was in any case too heavily built for long-distance cycling: at 1600 hours precisely the first stabs of pain warned him that his legs were becoming muscle-bound. He pulled into the roadside by a little hill which stood out abruptly from the flatness of the moors land surrounding it. About three hundred yards further on was a disused brickworks with a big smouldering kiln like a brown igloo and a little tin corrugated-iron office with the door boarded up and windows broken. There was a dirt road by the brickworks; he wheeled his bicycle down it, then, ~~went-behind the-hill~~ seeing a ~~copse-of-scraggy-trees-behind-the-hill,....~~ a grove of ~~scraggy-trees~~ beeches behind the hill, went into ~~them~~ their shade.

He put his bicycle down carefully then massaged his legs. His face was beginning to sting with the sun and the wind and ~~it-was~~ he was glad ~~cool-in-the-shade~~ of the shade of the trees. He took his sandwiches out and began to eat, a little guiltily, but with great enjoyment. The hill rose very steeply past the beeches and there were several clumps of bushes to the east, hiding whoever was in the grove completely from

166

sight of the road. He looked at his map and found that he was
at the foot of Sparrow Hill about two miles north of the centre
of Warley. He had only to reach the crest of the next hill and
it was downhill all the way. He finished his sandwiches and
lit a cigarette, smoking it rather furtively. ~~No-one could
see him, and~~ The only person who could possibly have objected
was Charles, who was to have shared this expedition with him.
But Joe was grateful that no-one could see him: he felt ob-
scurely that he'd let Lawrence down.

A scene came into his mind. Lawrence in his colonel's
uniform with the red tie and one pip missing was ~~speaking to~~
facing him in his tent. There was a meal on the lacquer table;
Lawrence had just raised a cup of coffee to his lips as Joe
came in. He looked very sad. 'I've asked too much of you,' he
was saying. 'Here, ~~eat~~ share this meal ~~for~~ with me.' 'No,'
Joe was saying, 'I don't want it.' Then he fell forward in
a dead faint across the lacquer table, and Lawrence saw the red
patch over his heart where the Turkish bullet had stuck him.

After he'd finished the cigarette he began to feel
thirsty. He started to ~~make~~ construct a scene about this--
        a Sam Browne for a sling
stumbling forward in the desert with ~~a bandage over his head,~~
supporting
~~holding~~ Lawrence with his good arm--but the thirst was too
actual and the ~~need~~ anticipation for satisfying it too great
a pleasure for him to continue. He looked at his watch and
then at the map again. Both actions were unnecessary, but part
    happiness
of the ~~pleasure~~ which was beginning to come over him.

He wheeled the cycle to the road, mounted it, but did
not start straightaway. The only sounds were the wind in the
telegraph wires and a ~~peewit~~ curlew's petulant cry in the

distance. But the wind didn't seem to have its usual note of
desolation and the curlew wasn't telling him to go back. He
was at the highest point in Warley now; the descent to the
valley began at the next hill.

It wasn't a very steep hill, but he put his three-
speed into bottom gear. He wanted very much to reach the top
of the hill and yet he didn't want to hurry it. The image did
not occur to him then--he was only seventeen, sex was a half-
shameful ~~thundersto~~ thunderstorm, a shambling miracle with a
face that never was the same--but it was like the first time
one undresses a woman. He was frightened. Frightened not so
much of what he would see as frightened of being disappointed;
frightened, too, of a new state of being, after which everything would be different.

When he reached the top of the hill he engaged top
gear and swooped down the other side with a few turns of the
pedals. Sparrow Hill Road is a ~~succession~~ switchback succession of hills going further and further down into Warley; his
speed carried him to the top of the next, giving him a Big
Dipper sensation in his groin as the ~~byci~~ bicycle nearly left
the road at the crest by Brigg's Farm. The sensation so
overwhelmed him ~~had~~ that he swerved barely in time to avoid a
patch of oil on the crown of the road. He wasn't frightened,
~~physical-courage-he-had-plenty-of,-physical-courage-of-the~~
~~cold,-businesslike-kind.--But-but-he-slowed-down-into-the-side~~
~~of-the-road.~~ but he came off the crown of the road and curbed
himself into a safer speed. ~~It-suddenly-occured-to-him,-too,~~
~~that-Lawrence-might-have-still-been-living-if-he-hadn't-been-so~~
~~fond-of-sensations-like-the-drug-he'd-just-been-taking-at-Brigg's~~

168

WRITING A NOVEL

~~Parm.~~

~~There was~~ Warley **was** is in the centre of a bowl of
arable land, with the moors to the north and Warley Forest to
the south. The River Merton, a tributary of the Wharfe, enters
through Squirrel Pass, a heavily wooded gorge about ~~two miles
west~~ of the Market Square. The industrial quarter is in the
east. There are two parks--St. Clair Park, which begins where
Sparrow Hill Road ends, and Snow Park, down by the river. St.
Clair Park was the old estate of the St. Clair family, who once
were the lords of the manor.
~~owned all of Warley that was worth owning.~~

The switchback levels out into at St. Clair road
which begins at the Park St. Clair Road ~~is a long steep descent
into Warley~~ descends in an almost straight line to ~~M Warley~~
Market Street, the town's main thoroughfare. It is dominated by
                    an artificial ruin of the Gothic Revival.
the St. Clair Folly, ~~a sandstone building of about fifty feet
high with a ground plan in the shape of an S and six S-shaped
stained glass windows on each side.--The roads leading off Sine
St. Clair Road.~~ The roads off ~~Sine~~ St. Clair Road--Linnet
Avenue, Dove Lane, Eagle Road, Cyprus Avenue, Lime Walk-- are
where most of the rich in Warley live~~.~~

Joe didn't see all this, of course. His main impression was trees and big houses and the sound of church bells. As
he came into the Market Street he heard the band in Snow Park.
It was the Stars and Stripes; after hearing it at that particular
time and place he was never again able to hear anyone fitting
facetious words to it. Be kind to your web-footed friends.
Even a duck has a mother--without a sense of outrage. **He**
~~particularly noticed Cyprus Avenue~~ One thing particularly
impressed him; as he passed Cyprus Avenue on his way down St.

169

John Braine

Clair Road, he saw that it was broad and straight and lined

with cypresses. The street where he lived in Dreffield was
                          didn't curve one inch
called Oak Crescent. It ~~was dead straight~~ and there wasn't even

even a bush along it. ~~Cyprus Avenue remained in his mind as a~~

~~symbol of Warley--it was as if like the difference between~~

~~real breasts and the sponge rubber kind.~~ Cyprus Avenue re-

mained in his mind as a symbol of Warley--it was as if all his

life he'd been eating sawdust ~~instead of bread~~ and thinking it

was bread. Thinking of bread made him feel hungry again.

He rode along Market Street into Market Square and

pulled up beside ~~Munge~~ Riley's Café. There was a smell of

frying ~~fish~~ meat from the café, mixed with the market's apples

and linoleum and cabbage stalks and sawdust. As he turned the

combination lock on his front wheel he swayed a little with
fatigue
~~hunger.~~ He put his hand against the wall to steady himself;
                                    it was as if some
the dizziness passed, but for a second ~~the market square had~~
barrier had been taken away
~~a strange sharpness.~~ Everything became intensely real; he was

watching himself in a ~~documentary~~ film someone else had made.
                                    clear
It was like a good documentary, accurate, sharp, with none of

the more obvious camera tricks, ~~it was so real that it was~~

~~unreal.--He had had these moments before~~ The black cobbles

splashed green and red and yellow with squashed fruit and

vegetables, a ~~moss gre~~ purple satin quilt held up high by a big

man in his shirt-sleeves, a pile of brightly-coloured women's

underwear with a giggle of young girls around it, the bells and

the music, a small girl in a blue sundress with one strap fast-

ened with a safety-pin--everything was significant, yet neither

more nor less than itself. There were no tricks with the lens

or the microphone, the buildings and the ground steadily obeyed

170

perspective, the colours didn't spill over into each other, the
sounds he heard were neither a symphony nor a discordance.
~~Nothing-was-unreal~~ Not one inch, one shade, one decibel, was
false; he felt as if he'd never ~~seen~~ used his senses at all
before and then, turning into the café ~~without-his-knowing-or-
wishing-or-regretting-it-the-barrier-came-down-again~~ he was
back to normality like a ~~skier~~ ski-jumper coming to earth.

Riley's Café is a single large room with ~~marble-
topped-tables-and~~ a service hatch at the far end. The owner,
Matt
~~Joe~~ Riley, was serving when Joe came in. He was six foot high
and weighed fifteen stones and was just beginning to run to fat.
His black hair was glistening with oil and set into suspicious-
ly regular waves and he was wearing green suede shoes, green
linen trousers, a red silk shirt and a broad yellow tie with a
pattern of red rickshaws. He had a big gold snake ring on his
right
~~left~~ hand and a gold signet on his left, and his watch had a
gold mesh bracelet. He had been, I discovered later, a moder-
ately successful professional boxer and still walked lightly on
the balls of the feet, though his own weight and long hours of
standing in the café were beginning to break down his arches.

The café was crowded with farmers and their wives,
stiff in blue serge and white starch and prickly straw hats,
eating big helpings of beef and sausage and ham and pickles.
Joe couldn't see a vacant seat and was turning to leave the
place when Riley came over to him. 'You're not after leaving
now, surely to God,' he said in an Irish brogue which, though
Joe didn't know it then, was only assumed in business hours;
Riley was born and bred in Warley and spoke normally with a
Warley accent, a softer variant of the West Riding accent.

'There's nowhere to sit,' said Joe. 'Indeed and there is.' He
took Joe to a table by the window. 'Herbert here's leaving this
very minute. There's not another drain to be had out of the
teapot and he's just eaten the last bit of bread-and-butter ~~that~~
~~I-meant-for-four-people~~. 'Howd this din,' said Herbert, a small
man in black leather leggings and a white starched shirt and
stiff collar with no tie. 'Howd this din and don't show me up
before this young gentleman, or Ah'll sup up t' vinegar and take
away tha cutlery too.' He pulled out a wallet stuffed with notes.
'Suppose Ah'd better gi' tha some brass.' He rose to his feet
and went over to the cash-desk. Joe took his place and looked
at the menu. ~~He-seemed-to-have-burnt-up-the-energy-from-the~~
~~'I-wouldn't-have-fish-and-chips-if-I-were-you,'~~
~~sandwiches-already;-he-visualized-his-stomach-as-an-engine~~
~~Riley-said,--Fish-isn't-a-thing-I-recommend-in-hot-weather~~
~~boiler-needing-protein~~
'By God, I'm hungry,' he said. 'What do you recommend?' He
was already beginning to pick up the right way ~~of-dealing-with~~
to order a meal, though ~~shyness~~ self-consciousness or a waiter's
indifference sometimes prevented him from bring it off. Riley
seemed pleased with Joe's question. 'Well,; he said, 'I wouldn't
recommend the fish. It's fresh, mind you, but a hungry man
wants something more solid. I've a beautiful ~~piece~~ bit of
inlift, I've beaten it tender with me own hands. How about a
big ~~piece~~ cut out of that with some onions and chips?' It was
then that Joe made a decision which, though a small one (a meal
is food, not a Holy Communion) was ~~an~~ extremely important. 'No onions or
chips, ~~he-said--'And-no-bread,-it~~ answered please,' he said. 'And just
a slice of dry bread.'

   It was important because it wasn't a thing he'd have
thought of asking for in Dreffield. In the few cafés there one
took exactly what was on the menu; it was as if cows had onions

potatoes
and ~~chips~~ embedded in their flesh at birth and fish swam the sea
coats of
in batter with swarms of chips around them. It was an act

of sensuality too; he liked meat much more than vegetables.
in Arabia
And, ~~still~~ the part of him which was still ~~well-in-the-desert~~

felt that ~~meat~~ he was having the kind of meal which Lawrence

would have had; the meat could have been broiled ~~that-morning~~

over a camp-fire and cut up with a jewelled dagger.

'You're a man of taste,' said Riley. 'Ive never seen

myself why anyone should be spoiling good meat with ~~masses~~ great

gobs of potatoes and onions. I'll order it this very minute.

Would you like a pot of tea while you're waiting?'

The tea was ~~black-hht~~ freshly made and strong. Joe

sat sipping it and looking out of the window whilst from the

kitchen came the smell of frying steak. He had never been as

happy in his whole life.

His table was a small one with only his chair at it;

it was placed against the window, a long ~~high-one~~ curved one

rather like a ship's bridge. It shouldn't have fitted in with

the Market Square, but it did. The café was at the top of the

square; his table was in the centre of the window, so he could
streets
see all the ~~roads~~ which led into it. Market Street was the
three
broadest, forming one side of the square; ~~two~~ other streets,

narrow and winding and cobbled, ran off it, one at each corner

of the cafe, ~~another-the~~ another, scarcely wide enough to take
people
two abreast, halfway up the left side. The two houses facing

each other at the end nearest the square were half-timbered;

Joe ~~knew-enough-about-architecture-to~~ recognised them as gen-
part
uine Elizabethan, with the beams an intregal of the structure

instead of laths nailed to plaster. There was a little bridge

173

John Braine

of wrought iron and glass connecting the two houses behind; it
seemed to be all that prevented the two sides of the street from
sagging towards each other. The name of the street had been
obliterated with great daubs of black paint.

'What's ~~s-the-name-of~~ ^{do they call} that street?' he asked Riley when
he brought the steak. Riley laughed. It was a deep infectious
laugh, but a little too professional; Joe noticed that his pale
blue eyes never changed expression. 'Well, ~~l-he's~~ 'That's a
vexed question,' he said. 'Officially its Elizabeth Street. On
account of the houses and the chairman of the Council's wife.'

'What did it use to be called?'

'Hangman's Lane. You see that house to the left?
That's where Jack Fletcher lived. No-one knows much about him--
it's nearly four hundred years ago--but some say he wasn't the
proper hangman but just a kind of assistant. He was a butcher,
like our present Chairman. His name's Fletcher too, and I
wouldn't be surprised if they weren't relations.'

'Has he the same shop?' asked Joe.

'It'd make a good story, but Fletcher's old house is a
draper's now. It's some of the people who live in Hangman's Lane
that put him up to it. They say the name's ugly and gives a
wrong idea of their moral character and ~~a-lot-more-blather~~ so on.
They don't see that you can be a devil fiend in Paradise Alley
and a wolf in Lamb Street and they don't see that the name's historical and brings visitors. Anyway, the newspapers got hold of
it, and now there's all sorts of societies playing the devil
with the chairman.'

'It's a good name for the street,' said Joe, beginning
his steak. It was three inches thick and nearly filled the

174

plate, and as he cut into it he saw that it was red at the heart.
'There's a lot of history in the town,' said Riley. 'You'd need
a lifetime here to know the half of it.' A man at the other end
of the room called his name ~~to him~~, and he padded over to him.
~~'Don't forget now, let me know how you enjoyed your~~ 'Enjoy your
steak now,' he said over his shoulder as he went.

Joe ate slowly, feeling his strength return with each
mouthful. As he ate, he kept his eyes on the market-place. The
shadows were lengthening now and The shadow of the big man sell-
ing bedspreads was lengthening now, ~~long~~ becoming angular and
Byzantine; the crowds ~~round the stalls~~ were diminishing and
~~most of~~ the stallholders were ~~drinking tea~~ bringing out thermos-
flasks and packets of sandwiches. He wondered ~~why Warley should
be found all that he saw~~ what was so extraordinary about Warley,
he tried to analyse the happiness which had settled over him
like an expensive camelhair coat--in a warm, ~~protective~~ solid
happiness that was at the same time as light and ~~sensual~~ senuous
as silk. He had been to towns as beautiful--Skipton, Otley,
Harrogate
~~Beverly~~, Ilkley--if not more beautiful. In fact, he'd been to
                          Yorkshire.
all the showplaces in ~~the west Riding~~. He had enjoyed them,
but they had been, he realised now, only excuses for a cycle run.
Warley was, though he hadn't known it when he set out that morning, a destination. What was happening to him in Riley's Café
that August afternoon was a marriage. The meal before him was
in itself only a meal; but his eating it at that time and place--
even if it had been stale buns instead of ~~cakes~~ steaks and the
                 tea   twice brewed
usual British café ~~brew~~, lukewarm and ~~used up~~ with a pinch of
soda for strength--was a ~~housewarming, a first meeting, the
first act of love in the new oak bed~~ housewarming, a commemoration.

John Braine

When he had finished his meat, cleaning his plate
with the bread, a girl brought him ~~a-piece-a~~ cheese and biscuits
and a fresh pot of tea. He used the whole pat of butter on one
biscuit, then spread it thickly with cheese. It was the strong
yellow Canadian kind; he ate it quickly, deliberately stinging
his palate, then poured himself another cup of tea and lit a
cigarette. ~~Besides-a-sol~~ Parked ~~opposite~~ by a solicitor's office
to the left of the café there was a green Aston-Martin tourer,
low-slung, with cycle-type wings and an air of speed and durabil-
ity. As Joe looked at it a young man ~~in-a-pair-of-brown-trousers~~
~~and-a-green-checked-shirt-crossed-the-road~~ and a girl crossed
the road and took their places in it. The yound man was just
~~lea-turning~~ about to turn the ignition key when the girl said
something to him, and after a moment he put ~~the-winds-aero-~~
~~sereens-down-and~~ the windshield up. The girl put out her hand
and smoothed his hair. Joe found the gesture ~~arotically~~ sexually dis-
turbing in a way which was difficult to explain, mixed up with
the steak and the expens low neck of her dress and the late
afternoon sun and the clean lines of the Aston-Martin; it was
again as if a barrier had been removed, but this time by an act
of reason. The ownership of the car put the young man in a
different world; ~~from-Joe~~ but ownership was simply a question
of money. The girl too, with even sun-tan and her fair hair
cut short in a style which looked too simple to be anything else
but expensive, was in a different world; ~~too~~ but her possession,
Joe realised, was the price of the diamond ring on her left hand.

The girl put on a blue Paisley head-scarf and the car
started with a deep healthy roar. As it turned into the direction of St. Clair Road Joe noticed the young man's ~~white~~ olive

WRITING A NOVEL

linen shit ~~with the~~ and brown silk ~~scarf tucked~~ neckerchief
~~around~~ fastened with a bone ring. The shirt was, somehow, worn
easily; everything about the young man was easy and loose,
but not tired and sloppy. He had an undistinguished face with
a narrow forehead and mousy hair cut short and tousled with the
wind. It was a rich man's face, smooth with good living and
shaving-lotion.

Joe had seen shirts and neckerchiefs like the young
man's in shops in Harrogate and Leeds; the shirt alone would
cost as much as all his the clothes he was wearing. Although
his happiness had not diminished, although the man and the girl
and the car were in a way part of that happiness, he felt for
a moment grubby and sweaty, ~~his hair itchy with hair oil and too~~ and juvenile.
~~long on top, too short at the back and sides.~~

~~He felt the beginnings of envy~~ For a moment the
sourness of envy gripped him, then he rejected it. Even at
that age, he had no time for envy. He felt ~~dimly but strongly~~
inarticulately that it was a small but deadly vice, as weaken-
ing as masturbation is supposed to be, and on the same plane--
the convict sulking because someone's got more skilly.

His rejection of envy didn't ~~lessen the~~ abate the
fierceness of his longing. He wanted a car like the Aston-
Martin, he wanted a two-guinea linen shirt, he wanted a girl
with a South of France suntan; he wanted a different world
from Dreffield. Without knowing it he had always wanted a
different world from Deffield; he had never, though he was born
and bred there, felt that he belonged to it. It was a dreary
little town in a succession of dreary little towns; its main
manufacture was textiles, the dependence on which had made its

John Braine

life a charade on Hard Times. It was situated in a wet little

               situation   the woods around it were

valley, its ~~terrain~~ a parody of Warley; ~~with-its-trees~~ chopped

down and built-up and the river which ran through it was a dirty

harlequin with dyes and textile waste. No-one in the town had

much money; like its two biggest mills were owned by a London

financial combine, and the its few executives and professional

                                                      was

~~people~~ men ~~there-were~~ mostly lived outside it. ~~It~~ There ~~was~~

~~dead~~ an ornate Carnegie library with a huge reading-room where

old-age pensioners dozed, a small park with the swings locked

up on Sundays, a railway station closed for passenger traffic

~~for-tw-since~~ twenty years back, its automatic machines empty,

its tin advertisements for cocoa and tea cracked and peeling,

~~There-wasn¹t-much-else~~ a small cinema ~~with-pillars-for~~ smelling

of stale pine disinfectant, a couple of farms which were not

farms at all, but milk and egg factories; ~~schools-with-asphalt~~

~~playgrounds,-Twopenny-Nan,-the-town¹s-one-prostitute-prostitute~~

three Board Schools almost identical in appearance, with asphalt

playground and ~~spik~~ savagely spiked ~~railway~~ railings, a Grammar

School like a larger and more ornate Board School, and ~~an-extra-~~

~~ordinary-number-of-public-urinals~~ a cast-iron ~~War~~ war memorial,

a copy of the Cenotaph, which had an oddly phallic appearance.

The council was mainly composed of shop-keepers and trade-union

officials, with two school-teachers and a Methodist parson co-

opted on the Library Committee. The executives and professional

men formed a tight little social circle of their own, mostly

                                                booked

taking their amusements in Leeds. ~~The-cinema-was-taken-each-~~

~~year-for-The-Messiah,-and-in-the-winter-the-Methodist-and~~

~~Wesleyan-dramatic-societies-plodded-steadily-through-Abe-Heywood¹s~~

~~catalogue.---There-wasn¹t-much-else-in-Dreffield,-unless-one-counted~~

178

~~the-public-conveniences,-a-sandstone-building-with-a-green-tiled~~
~~roof.~~ There were occasional political meetings, ~~in-the-cinema~~,
and ~~every~~ from September to April the Methodist and Wesleyan
Dramatic societies plodded steadily through Abe Heywood's dramatic catalogue. Whatever social life there was in Dreffield
was centred in the Nonconformist churches: Joe, who had a
pleasant voice and almost no self-consciousness, would rather
have liked to have done some acting, but his mother, an old-
fashioned rationalist of the Thinker's Library type, would have
been hurt--worse still, coldly contemptuous if he had involved
himself in any way with organised religion. ~~So-Dreffield~~ So
there was nothing for him in Dreffield. In the private vocabulary which he and Charles had evolved, it was Dead Dreffield,
and the councillors and officials and anyone they didn't like
were called zombies. ~~the-chairman-of-the-Council-was-Zombie~~
~~Number-one,-Charles'-Boss,-the-Chief-Librarian,-Zombie-Number~~
~~Two,-the-headmaster-of-the-Grammar-School-Zombie-Number-Three~~
~~beginn-and~~ It was a point of honour with them never to use
names but numbers. 'Zombie Number Two,' Charles would say referring to his boss, the Dreffield Librarian, ~~had-his-book-fund~~
~~cut-again.--He-pretended-to-be-angry,-but-zombies-have-no~~
~~feelings.'-spilt-his-tea-this-morning,-right-on-his~~ 'made a joke
                                                      pretend
this morning. It's pathetic, ~~the-way-how~~ when they ~~try~~ to be
alive.' After ~~the~~ Zombie Number Ten it became rather difficult
to remember whom they meant, so they used another system. 'The
Fat Zombies been watering the beer again,' Joe would say as the
landlord of the Dreffield Arms waddled by. 'He didn't come by
the new shroud honestly.' ~~Some-of-the-names-they-gave-to-people~~
~~in-Dreffield-they-found-oddly-frightening~~ There were times

179

when they almost took the whole business seriously; they once

saw the Smiling Zombie, who managed a big grocery, reduce

muscular

Bodger Collins (~~an-undersized-boy-whom-they-used-to-raid-or-~~

lumbering

~~chards-with~~), a ~~big~~ Irish boy who was something of a boxer,

to tears because of a mistake with an order. Bodger, who

could have picked up the Smiling Zombie with one hand, was

cowering away from him, ~~it-was-a-they-never-quite-forgot-his~~

~~red-blubbered-big-red-face-blubbered-with-tears-and-the-pale~~

~~venomousness-venom~~ his back against the counter and his head

sagging; they never forgot his look of shame and defeat.

What made it worse was that the Smiling Zombie had just re-

turned from his holiday and his usually pale face was mottled

and peeling with sunburn. 'Zombies don't take care of their

bodies,' Charles said. 'Did you notice he didn't even have

the decency to shout and swear at poor Bodger?'

 ~~But~~ Fundamentally it was all a joke, an organised

irreverence; Dreffield was only dead because of its initial

letter, just as Leeds was lecherous and Bradford boozy. ~~As-he~~

~~watched-out-of-sight-the-tail-end-of-the-Aston-Martin-with-its~~

~~white-G.B.-plated~~ But as he watched the tail-end of the Aston-

Martin with its shiny new G.B. plate go out of sight he real-

ised with a shock that Dreffield was, as far as he was concern-

ed, really dead. He enjoyed his ~~work-at-the-accountants'~~

work   the

~~office,-Smith-and-Winters,-the-accountant's-job-they-at-Smith~~
Treasurer's Department, but the Council's idea of salary
~~and-Winters,-the-accountants,-but-there-was-no-future-in-it,~~
scales wasn't generous and he could forsee the time when he'd
~~Smith-had-a-fourteen-year-old-son-who-was-good-at-figures,-and~~
grow tired of waiting for dead men's shoes.
~~Winters,-a-clever-and-tough-young-man-from-Bradford,-had-only~~

~~had-only-just-entered-the-partnership.~~

 Joe thought of the secondhand Austin Seven which

Treasurer
Tompkins, the ~~chief~~ deputy ~~clerk~~, had just bought. That was

the most Dreffield had to offer him: it wasn't enough. He

made the choice there and then. He wanted Warley. He wanted

two-guinea
the world of the Aston-Martin and the ~~made-to-measure~~ shirt,

of steak and cypresses and big houses and Hangman's Lane. He

was at exactly the right age to make the choice--to be aware,

in fact, that there was a choice. If he had been younger he

would have been unable to discriminate--all sports cars, all

pretty women would have been objects of desire. If he'd been

older, there would have been a thousand preoccupations to ob-

scure his view; it is even doubtful whether he would have

ridden as far as Warley.

If Charles had been with him, things would have been

different, too. They had at that time ~~worked-discovered-a~~

~~way-of-avoiding-envy~~ a special way of conversation to dispel

envy and its obverse, slavish admiration. 'The rotten sod,'

Charles would have said. 'Hope he gets a puncture.' 'Put

her clothes back on, Hopkins,' Joe would have said. 'The poor

girl hasn't a stitch on, her tits are turning blue.' 'Those

big pop eyes of yours are glinting with lechery,' Charles

would have said. 'Is it the car or the woman, though?' They

would have continued like that for some time; they generally

ended in laughter. It was a way of conversation which was an

incantation, a ritual: ~~it-was-effective-enough-as-far-as-its~~

~~main-purpose-was-concerned~~ the frank admission of envy ~~somehow~~

~~cleansing~~ cleansed them of it. And the outrageousness of

their remarks made them feel rakes, men-of-the-world. But the

incantation would have worked too well: it would have hidden

the fact that it was possible to reject Dreffield and choose

181

Warley. Then there was the Lawrence cult. Joe felt rather
shame-facedly, glad that Charles was at home with the shingles.
He didn't want to discuss, for the hundredth time, what exactly
happened to Lawrence when the Turks captured him. He didn't
wish to plan an attack on Warley, to mark out strongpoints
with coloured pins on the map. ~~He wanted, in fact, to be alone.~~
He had a more ~~exciting~~ important campaign to plan.

An excitement came over him. It was entirely adult;
he'd never felt anything like it before. ~~Warley was the kind
of place one would dream of in Dreffield.~~ Warley was so much
different from Dreffield that it was like a dream. But it
wasn't a dream. It was real. He could go inside the dream,
he could live in it. He didn't plan except in the vaguest most
general terms--a job in Warley, to ~~least his A.C.C.A. Inter~~ pass his examinations
because the excitement was too strong. He was like an officer
fresh from ~~the~~ training school, unable for the moment to translate the untidiness of fear and cordite fumes into the obvious
irresistible text-book attack. After the excitement came a
momentary depression: the meal he had just eaten was an ex-
travagance, Riley would be laughing at his affectation of
maturity, Dreffield and his mother's reproaches for being so
late lay fifty miles ahead of him. As the young officer might
forget that the confusion of trees and corpses and machine-gun
fire ahead of him was Hill 606, easily captured from its north
flank and the key to the whole situation, so he forgot the personal assets which guaranteed ~~what he wanted~~ in themselves almost his desires.

He looked at his watch with the usual flourish and
discovered that it was nearly half-past five. He signalled to
Riley, who came over straightaway. 'Was everything to your

liking?' he asked.   'I've never enjoyed a meal more,' Joe said.
Riley's heavy features split into a smile. 'That's what I like
to hear,' he said. He lowered his voice. 'Some of these people
remind me of a story my grandmother told me about a woman who
cooked grand meals for her menfolk for thirty years and never
had one word ~~from~~ of praise from them. And one day[1]-he leaned
closer to Joe and there was a whiff of talcum and violet-oil ~~of~~
~~violets~~ and whisky and cloves--'when they lifted the covers
from their dinner-plates there was nothing but little heaps of
straw there. "What the devil ~~do-you-mean~~ are you at, woman?"
the man of the house bellowed, "giving us straw for our dinner?"
"I might as well have been serving straw," says she "for all
the notice you've taken these thirty years; so you can eat
straw now and like it, for I'm cooking no more."' Joe threw
his head ba~~x~~k and laughed heartily: he had a pleasant, deep
laugh, in which only Charles was able to detect a note of
falsity, the light opera touch as he called it.

          Riley gave Joe his check in a curiously furtive way.
~~As~~ 'There's no hurry to be going,' he said. 'We don't close
till ~~seven~~ten, unlike some places I could name.' As Joe picked
up the check, a spasm of cramp ran through his legs and he
winced. 'Don't tell me it's the bill that's upsetting you,'
said Riley. Joe smiled. ~~He-had,-for-his-age,-a-mature,-hard~~
~~face-faintly-worried.~~ He had a mature face for his age: the
full lips were held tightly and his eyes had a watchful expression. When he smiled his eyes became defenceless and
friendly and his cheeks creased into two lines which were too
long to be dimples and too short to reach the nostrils and give
the smile ~~an~~ a ventriloquist's dummy rigidity. He had ~~dis~~

John Braine

known for some time that his smile almost always made people ~~do-things-for-him~~ confer, ~~favours-upon-him,~~ or want to confer, favours upon him. He used it this time with no other motive than to be agreeable. 'The bill's most reasonable.' he said. 'I've come fifty miles today, though. Too far, to judge ~~my the~~ by the state of my legs.' Riley leaned down and touched Joe's calf lightly. 'You've a better build for boxing than cycling.' he said. 'If you'll wait a moment I'll get you something for that stiffness.' 'Thank you very much,' said Joe, and smiled again.

As Riley went upstairs to his office he found himself wondering why he should inconvenience himself. I feel as if he'd given me a big tip, he thought. A good-looking boy, but there's something else. ~~I-can't-put-my-finger-on~~ One can't help liking him. ~~he-picked-up-the-bottle-of-lini- ment.~~ He took the bottle of liniment from the cupboard above his desk, and paused for a moment, his thick fingers drumming the dusty wood. ~~He-had-exchanged-for-his-ring instincts~~ 'What the hell,' he said aloud, 'it's only half-a-bottle of liniment.' He wrapped the bottle up in an old copy of The Ring and went downstairs.

'Rub this well in,' he said to Joe, 'all over your calves and thighs. Don't sit around afterwards, but get moving straightaway.' Joe started to fumble in his pocket. 'No, no,' said Riley quickly. 'You couldn't buy it anyway. I make it up myself for the boys at the Athletic Club. It'll take you home, I promise you.' 'I'll do that,' said Joe. "Thank you again, Mr. Riley.' He was searching for words; it was extremely important, he felt, that he chose the right ones.

184

'I've never had a better day or a better meal.' He rose and
shook Riley's hand. The words and the gesture were entirely
sincere; but there was a part of him, like a professional
producer watching a gifted amateur company, which found the
words a little too gushing, the handshake a little too clumsy,
and made notes for the futures.

'It's nothing at all,' said Riley. 'Come again,
and I'll have something special for you.' 'I'll come again,'
said Joe, as he paid his bill, and walked out into the market
square.

Despite the liniment and the talk of fifty miles,
he had almost forgotten his bicycle. ~~There-was~~ He half-
expected to find a car waiting for him; the bicycle was an
anti-climax, a reminder of Dreffield, where nearly all the
young men owned ~~bicycles~~ one. He ~~unlocked~~ unfastened the
combination lock which he had set at DEATH. As the last
letter clicked into place the word struck him as being childish.
He wasn't going to die: the idea was particularly at this
time and place, indecent.

He ~~cycled~~ rode down Market Street towards Squirrel
Gorge. The River Merton is a half-loop to the south of Warley,
with Warley Forest behind it. Snow Park is between the river
and the Forest. The park narrows past Market Square, ~~so-that~~
~~the-streets~~ as if to let the forest come nearer, so that the
streets end in running water and trees. The park broadens
out again by Squirrel Bridge, a quarter-of-a-mile from Market
Square. Its shape is roughly like a blind letter B turned
towards the town, with the playing-fields and boathouse in the
Squirrel Bridge half and the bandstand and gardens in the

John Braine

Market Square half.

   The boats were out and there was a sound of music
upstream
from ~~over the water~~. Roll out the barrel we've got the blues
on the run; but distance and running water gave the words an
odd wistfulness, they were the beginning of some...~~on the last~~
~~month of summer perhaps on the summer but more likely as he~~
~~thought long~~ perhaps on the summer. The river smelt cool and
green and damp ~~dank~~ and the breeze which came off it goose-
pimpled his bare arms. A few hundred yards away was the old
Squirrel Bridge, a narrow humpbacked bridge dating from the
~~seventeeth~~ seventeenth century, unquestionably picturesque,
weathered into the soft grey of good worsted. The white con-
         beside it
crete of the new bridge was harsh ~~beside~~ and blaring ~~beside~~
~~and amongst the soft greens and browns around it~~ and the
streamlined buttresses, projecting an unusual distance beyond
the parapet, seemed to belong to aerodynamics rather than
      liked it very much
architectures. But Joe he ~~found in himself a great liking for~~
        being
~~it:~~ it was a sign of prosperity, that of Warley ~~was~~ unquestionably alive, it was the rich uncle from America, smelling of
cigars, scattering jobs and turkeys and bottles of wine--beside
it the other bridge was a poor relation, the ~~charming~~ spinster
aunt ~~who had to be charming because she had nothing else to~~
~~give~~ with no gifts but charm, and the desire to please.

   There was a house on the river bank, standing out
from the bungalows around it. It was so close to the bank that
he thought for a moment its foundations must be under the water
until he saw that is was built on pillars, its ground floor
beginning on the bridge level. A girl was sitting in the bay
window overlooking the river, a book in her hand. Her hair was

WRITING A NOVEL

As the taxi rode smoothly up the long hill I felt a
sudden joy. How lucky I am, I thought. All too easily I might
have had the wrong landlady, smelling of washing-soda and
faded gentility; I might have been ~~be-now-in-the-usual-boarding
house-room-the-ewer-and-handbasin-and-chamber-pot~~ in one of
those houses by the station, ~~with-the-sounds-of-the-engines
and-the-train-smoke~~ from one Dufton to another.

My main impression was trees and big houses and expensive cars; but what I remember best is Cyprus Avenue. That's
to the right, half-a-mile exactly from the bottom of St. Clair
Road. It's broad and straight and lined with cypresses.

world of the
I was going to the top, into the big houses and
trees...and the expensive cars and the wind coming from the
moors and woods on the skyline.

When Mrs. Thompson took me into my room I knew that
I was in a new world. 'It's marvelous,' I said, feeling the
inadequacy of the words.

It was at the Thompson's that I first learned about
pictures, a knowledge which has been extraordinarily useful to
me. It's surprising how many businessmen collect pictures;
in any case it's as good a topic as any when one's dirty stories
run out and one doesn't want to drink any more. Those who know
nothing about it generally think of one as a sensitive imprac-
tical type or a very interesting, artistic but a good fellow;
those who know a lot about it think of one as a kindred spirit
or someone to be taught what art is. All of which suppositions
can generally to turned to

so fair that it was nearly white, and she wore a bright scarlet
dress.

It was another nail in the coffin of Dreffield: When
he came into Squirrel Gorge with its steep sides covered with
pines and bracken and rocks and lively with children and ~~pick-
nickers-picnickers-and~~ little streams running into the river,
he was not leaving Warley to go home. He wasn't going to
Dreffield at all, he was going to his base for supplies; and
the tyres hummed over the tarmac, the details of the campaign
became clearer and clearer.

WRITING A NOVEL

(D) NOTES--SECOND DRAFT

Accrington brick--CI--remember you've already men-
tioned it when you do return to Dufton chapter.

In end: Mrs. T. telling Joe she answered his
advert .. had seen photo in paper, he was like her son &/or
Tordaff & someone told her he was like her son.

I'd fixed up lodgings through an advertisement in
the Warley Courier; I hadn't actually seen my landlady, Mrs.
Thompson. Even without the maroon coat and copy of the Queen
she said I'd recognise her by I knew who it was standing by the
barrier; she belonged to her notepaper, thick, white, hand-
woven, and her small clear handwriting.

We went out over a covered footbridge which shook as
a train went under it and through a long echoing subway.

Not that it was very evident from what I could see.
The station at Warley is in the middle of the industrial
quarter to the east, at the end of a long winding road leading
to the Market Square.

The station at Warley is in the centre of the eastern
quarter. Looking around me that morning, the effect was as if
all the industry and working-class had been crammed into this
one spot. Later I discovered that this was a matter of Council
policy: if you wanted to set up a heavy manufacturing business
in Warley, it was the east or nowhere.

She was the sort of person with whom one quickly
established intimacy, or never--if the Sunday papers haven't
dirited the word beyond use--and the intimacy was as cool and
dry but as friendly and firm as her handshake.

John Braine

It was raining from the west the morning I came to
Warley. The sky was the grey of Guiseley sandstone and the
sound of the rain against the carriage window ~~bricked-me-in,~~
~~as-it-were,~~ made me feel sleepy and vaguely frightened; when
the train stopped I didn't really want to leave it.

The sky was the grey of Guiseley sandstone and the
rain against the carriage window seemed to cut off all other
sounds. I was alone in the compartment. As the train slowed
down going into the station

The sky was the grey of Guiseley Sandstone and the
rain lashed the carriage window was driving venomously
against the carriage window.

The sky was the grey of Guiseley sandstone and the
rain lashed the carriage window with such venom that, as the
train slowed down for the station, I didn't really want to
leave it.

The sky was the grey of Guiseley sandstone and the
rain against the carriage window seemed to cut all other
sounds off, bricking me up in a world of my own.

The sky was the grey of Guiseley sandstone and I
felt an emptiness inside me.

The sky was the grey of Guiseley sandstone. I felt
faintly a sense of anti-climax and for

I had a sense of anti-climax.
I don't quite know what I'd expected--blue skies and

a red carpet perhaps., For a moment I didn't want to ~~go to~~
leave the train.
~~Warley at all.~~ I was alone in the compartment. I remember.

As the train slowed down going into the station I said to

myself: No more zombies, Joe, no more zombies.

The sky was the grey of Guiseley sandstone. I had

a sense of anti-climax and a momentary ~~and ridiculous~~ desire
        stay on
not to ~~leave~~ the train, half-awake and half-dreaming, the

sound of the rain walling me up in a seedily cosy world of no

decisions, no new faces, home or job. I wan alone in the

compartment. I

The sky was the grey of Guiseley sandstone, I felt

a sense of anti-climax. I don't quite know what I'd expected--

blue skies and a red carpet perhaps. I had a ridiculous mo-

mentary desire not to leave the train; after three hours'

travelling the compartment had assumed a seedy cosiness. The

train slowed down going into the station; I said firmly to

myself: No

        - I'd expected this arrival to have about it a fla-

vour of brass bands and red carpets and blue skies

The sky was the grey of Guiseley sandstone. I had a

sense of anti-climax: I suppose that, this being the most im-

portant day in my life, I'd expected the equivalent of blue

skies and red carpets and brass bands

The sky was the grey of Guiseley sandstone. I had a

sense of anti-climax. For a moment I didn't want to leave the

train; after three hours' travelling the compartment had assum-

John Braine

ed a seedy cosiness.

No more zombies, Joe, no more zombies, I said to
myself firmly as the train slowed

It was raining from the west the morning I came to
Warley. The sky was the colour of Guiseley sandstone. As the
train slowed down going into the station I had a sense of anti-
climax; somehow I'd expected something wonderful to happen,
something with the flavour of brass bands and red carpets.

It was raining from the west and the sky was the
~~colour~~ grey of Guiseley sandstone the morning I came to Warley.
It was the best

There are moments one wants to keep

I often think of the morning when I came to live in
Warley. Always I have that sense of brass bands and red carpets and blue skies.

Actually, it was raining heavily and the sky was the
grey of Guiseley sandstone.

I reached Warley at 10:30 a.m. exactly. It was raining from the west and the sky

If I were only allowed to keep one memory it would
be the moment the train slowed down going into Warley.

My stomach was rumbling with hunger and the drinks
of the night before had left a throbbing in my head and a
carbonated-water sensation in my nostrils.

If I were only allowed to remember one event I

should choose

If I were only allowed to remember one day of my life I should choose the day that I came to live in Warley.

It began on a wet September morning with the sky the colour of Guiseley sandstone. I was alone in the compartment as the train slowed down going into the station. I said to myself: No more zombies, Joe, no more zombies.

I once had to write a composition at school on the happiest day of my life.

This was something new: if ever I'd thought about pictures at all before coming to Warley, I'd thought of them as pieces of furniture. I knew, for instance, that there were three pictures in Aunt Elizabeth's living-room but I couldn't at that moment remember what their subjects were. ~~And she had, I was certain, always had the same pictures there~~ I am normally observant and I'd seen the pictures daily for two years and they had in any case been there ever since. Aunt Elizabeth was married. They were part of the surroundings, they weren't really meant to be looked at. The Medici prints were meant to be looked at. They belonged to a pattern of gracious living; to my surprise the tatty phrase straight from the women's magazines accurately conveyed the atmosphere of the room-- it was as if a ready-made suit fitted.
to my surprise--it was as if a ready-made suit fitted--the woman's magazine phrase conveyed the atmosphere of the room remarkably well.

I suppose it was homesickness, a childish desire

193

John Braine

never to leave the cosiness of familiar rooms and street, the
security of faces which might bore but never would betray

a childish~~ly~~ desire never to leave the rooms and streets
where one could never be lost, the people who might bore but
never would betray.

    I suppose it was homesickness, a childish desire
never to leave the ugly rooms and streets where to be hungry
or last wasn't possible, never to meet any but the familiar
people who might bore or ~~annoy~~ _{irritate} but not hurt or betray.

    My business is money: I can smell its presence
or absence, I've an instinct like a water-diviner's.

    I'm an accountant and I've an instinct about money

    I'm an accountant and I've an instinct like a water
diviner's about money; I can always sense its presence.

    'I'm so sorry,' she said. 'These dreadful wars--
we always seem to have been at war somehow...

    There were many more--we knew a lot about the citi-
zens of Dufton, more than the Incestuous Zombie and the Childloving Zombie thought that we did

    There were many more: we both knew a great deal
about the ~~citizens~~ people of Dufton--much more, for instance,
than the Incestuous Zombie and the Childloving Zombie thought
that we did.

    'Yes,' I said, 'I'll get over it, though.' ~~I real-~~

194

WRITING A NOVEL

~~ised-that~~ That sounds callous, I thought, and I was opening
my mouth to explain myself when she came to my rescue.

      'I know what you mean. Men's friendships are much
deeper than women's but men are much less possessive

When he'd left the room I
He looked up from a sheaf of papers (as I came in)
I said I'd better go and unpack
END: I was dead too, dead inside. I hadn't really escaped
from Dufton. You never did. I was a zombie too--the Success-
ful Zombie.

John Braine

JFK--The Turret--Air Gunners Association

Leeds......30/1/54

Chapter in Dorset--Alice meets Joe at Wool. She has a cottage near Lulworth Cove in a secluded bay. They swim and sunbathe, make love. It is then that her child is conceived. He remembers afterwards that her hand moved towards her handbag then away, as if precautions didn't belong with that world of sun and shingle and trodden turf and pagan well-being-- they would be ignoble and grimy there naked on the beach.

He feels that the child could have been nothing but good and wise and strong after that week of perfect happiness in that lush countryside, the Cerne Giant blessing them, lobsters fresh from the sea nourishing them, strong, dark beer in the little pubs, driving round in the Fiat, it coming to life too, being in that almost Mediterranean heat Toppolino, the mouse, chic and sexy, not the suburban Baby: not the technical 500.

? Rewrite Chapter 7 into big notebook? Write Bill Porter--you can't do the revue. You must write 60,000 words this month--they've got to be good.

He made love with the precision of a surgeon. She was fascinated by his hands--pale, smooth, with gleaming nails, they explored her body like intelligent animals. When she kissed them afterwards she was thanking them, not him--she didn't really care for that red pork-butcher's face, with its expression of mingled anger and sadness.

WRITING A NOVEL

It smelled damp in the theatre---There is a feeling
about a theatre at rehearsals that it's difficult to convey.
It's the emptiest, most silent place on God's earth: it's
mostly those rows of empty seats, like empty places at the
family table..At the same time you can't be bored, as long
as you're taking part in the production, even the time waiting round is somehow creative. This is the true reason for
amateur dramatics: besides that feeling, whatever pleasure
is given from the actual acting is trivial. I always felt
this when I was at the theatre; but when Alice was beside
me the pleasure was increased.

And the publicity display in the foyer, the school-
room smell, like flats stacked up on the stage, and the litter
of props, the card-tables stacked together for a dining
table, the chairs together for a sofa, were part of home...

Introduce this in the chapter...keep away from
bareness, take the reader in that car.

There's a special feeling about a theatre during
rehearsals.

During the second week of rehearsals Ronnie took
one act each evening. Alice didn't come on till the second
act, so I didn't see her till the Tuesday following.

There's a special feeling about a theatre during
rehearsals...

When Alice came to sit beside me the pleasure was
increased...

John Braine

(That Tuesday evening I'd not seen her since taking Susan to the ballet; Ronnie was devoting each evening to one act, and she didn't come on till Act 2. --Is this really necessary? Precisely what significance has it? The answer is: none. The Function of this chapter is to show how much he was beginning to <u>need</u> Alice, and how well they acted together, and how they came to be lovers. I'm not sure that I shouldn't omit the chapter at her house--in any case it would be most unwise of her. Let them become lovers in the Fiat at Sparrow Hill.

CUT the chapter where he makes love to her at her house.

CUT from the Sparrow Hill chapter all this flummery about Tuedays and so forth.)

The evening with Susan depressed me.

Susan's coldness depressed me all Sunday and even

Susan's coldness depressed me for some time afterwards. ~~It wasn't a tangible sort of depression--it was rather~~ like that dim sadness one experiences on waking from a dream of winning seventy-five thousand on the pools.

It was like that ~~gray~~ washing day sadness that comes to one on waking to the realisation that marriage to Arletty and the £75,000 cheque was just a dream after all.

Susan's coldness depressed me for some time afterwards. It wasn't a tangible sort of depression; it was rather like that washing-day sadness which comes to one on waking to the realisation that the £75,000 cheque, so real even its the tuppeny stamp, was just a dream, after all.

    I began to shake it off a little when I went to the
Thespians the following Monday. There's as atmosphere about a
theatre at rehearsals that's ~~curiously~~ ^{as} comforting as cloves
for toothache. It's dusty, it's dry, it has huge reservoirs
of silence into which all one/ ^{'s} words fall miserably;

    It's dusty, it's dry, it's chilly, it has, no matter
how much noise is being made, a huge reservoir of silence into
which all one's words seem to take belly-flops, and the rows
of empty seats seem like empty seats at a family party. But
at the same time it's warm and cosy and private, it's impossible
to be bored; as long as one's taking part in the play; even
waiting for one's cue is somehow creative and exciting, and
every activity has

    When Alice came to sit beside me this sense of plea-
sure was increased. A great wave of relief came over me; it
was like

But at the same time it's impossible to be bored as long as
one's taking part

    But at the same time it's warm and cosy and private
as a nursery and every activity, even just waiting for one's
cue, is important and exciting...

    When Alice came to sit beside me the sense of plea-
sure increased. For a moment I experienced a wild longing
that was half-lust and half-laughter.

    When Alice came to sit beside me the sense of

pleasure increased. I felt reassured, too, protected somehow
by her presence. It was how I'd feel when the Efficient
Zombie...humiliation. Except that I'd never wished to undress
Charles and, I thought with a considerable shock, I wanted to
undress Alice.

I didn't enjoy it very much. But afterwards talking with her with her arms around my neck and her shirt lying
in the back of the car I felt a great warmth and companionship

She wriggled out of the garment. Her mouth to my
ear, she asked me a question.
'Yes. Always.'

And we'll have her singing that song? NO

It wasn't the only important thing between us. I
somehow wish now that I'd kept her just as a friend. But I
am as I am, over-sexed; and she was as she was, loving but
never finding a man good enough.

I could get sex at any pub or dancehall but not the
friendship which Alice had given me right from that first
evening in the St. Clair. It had come to us quickly and smoothly but without hurry or hysteria: I remember her quoting
to me the bit from Mr. Polly about there being friendship at
first sight. "I felt it with you," she said. "Right from the
beginning." I've been told I'm handsome, that I'm a superb
lover but nothing has flattered me so much as that remark of
Alice's.

Man in pub: He's always singing. Not that he can

sing. He's one of them crooners, you know. Hair's always flopping in his eyes, he's I-Believing all day long. Married, two kids. Of course, his wife doesn't understand him, he's going with another girl. Hasn't left his wife, knows when he's well-looked after. He's yattering about it all day long. For Christ's sake, man, I says, either leave your wife or leave this girl, one or the other, but stop going on about it to me. But I love her, he says. Makes me want to spew, him and his I Believe, what a bloody tripey song...'

"It's good to see you,' I said and meant it. 'You too,' she said. When she smiled I could see that her teeth weren't very good: there was a speck of decay in one of the upper centre incisors and the light caught a filling that took up almost half of another. They weren't bad; but they were no better than mine and the fact gave me a kinship with her and the fact gave me a shabby but genuine kinship with her, like having had the same operation: there wouldn't be the same feeling
and the fact gave us a shabby but genuine kinship which I could never have with Susan: I loved to look at her teeth, white and regular and small, but they always gave me a sense of inferiority.

Susan--
'I do think that men have a nice/wonderful smell,' she says. 'Tobacco and stale beer and new cotton and sweat.'

To Susan--
'I've been shopping, kid. Do you like my new cap, kid?

201

Where are we going, kid? Are you keen on me, kid?'

'I know my lines now,' I said. 'I can say the Song
of Solomon bit backwards. It's <u>lush</u>.'

'We'll knock 'em in the aisles,' she said.

And that evening we put in such a good performance
that Ronnie didn't once have to correct us during our big scene;
there was even a faint ripple

And that evening we put up our best performance,

As a matter of fact, we were very good. That evening
I threw myself into my part with more than my usual enthusiasm.
It was near enough to my own experience for me to live it, and
remote enough from my own experience for it

As a matter of fact, we put up an extremely good performance that evening. ~~I was supposed to be an ambitious young~~
I expect it was a relief for me to pretend to be someone else,
to inhabit a world

As a matter of fact, we put up ~~an extremely~~ a first-
rate performance that evening. The part was near enough to my
own experience for me to understand it: I was supposed to be
an ambitious young farmworker who nearly throws away the
chance of a farm of his own because of his passion for an
~~an older woman. I could live the part, which, of course, isn't~~
~~the thing for a professional~~ a sophisticated and sexy woman
from the city

As a matter-of-fact, we put up a first-rate performance that evening

We were becoming very

As a matter of fact, we put up a first-rate performance that evening. I not only remembered all my words, but spoke them properly; and for the first time the moves began to make sense. ~~I'm not an actor, of course, but I was ideally cast.~~ Being big and beefy and redfaced and speaking with a Yorkshire accent helped; as Alice said afterwards, the author must have had me in mind.

As a matter of fact we put up a first-rate performance that evening. For the first time all the words and all the moves made sense

I went on stage

My cue came

When my cue came a moment later I ~~walked~~ didn't walk on to the stage. I made an entrance. I had to stand glowering at Herbert and Eva for a moment before I spoke. Up to that evening, I'd always ~~got it wrong~~ made a mess of it, either ~~being too long~~ holding the silence too long or not long enough. That evening I timed it perfectly. I knew instinctively that I had. And I knew that I'd ~~achieved~~ managed the right degree of sulleness, and I knew that the reason for the sulleness was that I was thinking of my mistress and was feeling like a tethered bull. Everything clicked into place, I couldn't go wrong; and when Alice came on, something happened which is rare with amateurs: we achieved exactly the right tempo; I found myself thinking, or

rather sensing, that at some places I must go slowly, and at others more quickly, and I sensed, too, that the slowness and
the quickness ~~weren't~~ hadn't, as it were, to be dumped in heaps but to be spread smoothly. And for the first time in my life, I became aware of my own voice and body not ~~conceitedly-but coldly-as~~ without conceit, as instruments. ~~Alice-was-Alice still,-but-just-as-the-hard~~ Alice was no more to me and no less, than ~~the-nurse~~ Theatre Sister to the surgeon; she wasn't Alice Ackroyd whom I'd just wanted to undress, she was the character in the play...

Sees Susan, is invited there for tea. Gets rid of Alice.

SYNOPSIS

Joe meets Bob and Eva Sykes at the Thompsons', and they go together to see a play at the Warley Thespians. ~~together~~ Susan Brown, the young daughter of a prosperous local manufacturer, is taking part in the play. He falls in love with her: at best, he visualises himself as Swineherd to her Princess. He joins the Thespians and is ~~cast-for-the~~ given a part in one of their plays. ~~His~~ He plays opposite Alice Ackroyd, ~~the-thirty-two-year-old-wife-of-a-woolman~~ an ex-professional actress and wife of a mill-owner.

He thinks her standoffish at first, but a genuine friendship grows up between them, and he confides a great deal more to her than ever he's done to anyone: he tells her about his feelings towards Susan and even his rebuff by Eva, who has led ~~him-on-and-then-turned-cold.---Susan-is-cold-towards-him, too,-but-not-in-the-same-way,-she-goes-out-with-him-occasionally~~

~~to~~ him to believe that she'll go share a weekend with him, then turned virtuous at the last moment. ~~Susan,-whom-he-doesn¹t-of course-think-of-seduces~~ Susan goes out with him occasionally and seems to enjoy his company, but apparently is unwilling to allow even the mildest manifestation of the physical to enter their relationship. And she ~~keeps-him-secret-from-her-parents doesn¹t-invite-him-home-for-tea,-in-fact,-she~~ doesn't, to say the least of it, ~~invite-him-to-her-home-for-tea~~ take him home to tea: in fact, he has the impression that she keeps their friendship hidden from her parents.

He discovers that Alice and her husband aren't very happy together. They become lovers during the run of the play: the act itself is at first no more than an extension of their friendship. They meet every week in the nearby city; Alice has the use of a flat there.

Joe stays at Dufton for Christmas. Charles advises him to ~~leave-its-Susan-alone-for-a-while.---If-she-wants-the affair-to-go-any-further,-she¹ll-stop-to~~ stop pursuing Susan for a while. If she still wants to see him, she'll take over the pursuit; if she doesn't care whether he's interested in her or not, then Joe will be saved the humiliation of rejection. Charles also advises him not to imagine himself in love with Alice. Joe's Aunt Emily advises him to be content with what he has and to marry a good girl of his own class.

He returns with relief to Warley and the Medici prints and the green-tiled bathroom and Alice. He adopts the tactics Charles has advised in regard to Susan, and, as he discovers by hearsay at a NAUO social, it has exactly the result he hopes for.

205

John Braine

He's not surprised when, at a party they're both invited to, she throws herself into his arms. This is Joe's ~~supreme-mo-triumphant~~ moment of triumph: he has an agreeable and intelligent mistress and a young and beautiful beloved. Because he has Alice very comfortably in bed, so as to speak, he's able to put Susan on a pedestal, to act out the fairy story.

Firstly, he quarrels with Alice. He finds himself more upset than this than he cares to admit, but reflects that he'll sooner or later be found out anyway, and it might spoil his chances with Susan.

Secondly, he's warned off Susan by the Chief Treasurer, who points out that Brown is very influential on the Council, and that, whilst he wouldn't have Joe sacked, he could quite easily hold up his promotion. Joe's frightened, then angry, and ~~resolves-to~~ continues to see Susan. ~~He-d~~ Doors begin to shut in his face. For instance, Bob and Eva Sykes, at whose house he and Susan have been baby-sitting, suddenly discover that they don't need baby-sitters after all.

~~Now-he's-cut-down-to-size.~~ He goes to the Civic Ball in a hired ~~dress~~ evening suit, which doesn't fit, and ~~sees,-to-his-chagrin,-that-Susan's-been-taken-to-the~~ watches Susan dancing with Jack Wales, a wealthy young man with whom Susan had an understanding before she met Joe. Jack's suit fits and he's bigger & better-looking than Joe. He reflects ~~that-one-of-the-most-unfair~~ that if only Nature knew anything about social justice she'd arrange for all rich men to be old, puny and ugly.

It isn't long before he returns to Alice. The

206

affair enters a new phase, becomes almost respectable, a kind

of marriage. ~~He thinks seriously~~ Susan is told about his un-

faithfulness by Eva. She tells him that she doesn't ever want

to see him again, and he's too fed-up with her--~~importunities~~

he finds her youthful exuberance too exhausting--to try to

keep her. She goes away to stay with friends in France.

Joe spends three days with Alice in Dorset--in retro-

spect the three best days of his life. He meets Charles in

London. Charles advises him to throw over Alice, and to ask

Susan to forgive him.

When they're both drunk, Charles helps Joe to write

a letter to Susan. Charles keeps the letter: Joe forgets

about it, it's just one of those things one ~~does when~~ thinks

of after the eighth pint.

Joe returns to Warley and resumes the affair with

Alice. He seriously contemplates going away with her and

resigning his job at the Treasurer's. He can't ~~manage with-~~

~~out her~~ live without her

                                      to lunch

Brown asks him ~~to see him~~ at the Conservative Club.

To Joe's surprise he offers him a job in his firm, and implies

that he gives his permission to marry Susan. The condition is

that he gives up Alice. Joe accepts. He sees Susan, and dis-

covers that Charles has posted the letter they wrote in London.

It has had the effect Charles said it would have. He should

be happy now but he isn't. Susan has, he realises, bought him.

Charles has taken it upon himself to run his life for him.

But he can't refuse the offer: it's everything that he ever

wanted. In Warley he meets Alice that evening and tells her

that the affair can't go on. She doesn't argue or plead with

him, but takes his the matter in what appears to him a cold
and matter-of-fact way. He's glad that she's so sensible
about it.

The next day he hears that she's been killed in a
car accident. After she left him, she went on a pub-crawl,
and went off the road at a village some twenty miles away
from Warley.

He goes to see her husband and discovers that she
was pregnant. The husband has never been jealous of Joe before, but he suddenly attacks him. Joe takes his blows without retaliation: his early upbringing reasserts itself and
he feels that he deserves it. He knows why the husband's
angry: he and Alice were never able to have children.

He wanders round Warley, shell-shocked with grief,
and then goes to the city nearby. He tours all the lowest pubs
and finishes up in a tough dancehall where he beats up three
youths who resent his picking up one of the girls there. Bob
& Eva Sykes come across him in the centre of Warley and take
him back to the Thompsons' in their car. She makes it plain
to him that she's now perfectly willing to take Alice's place:
the coldness of it sickens him.

When he returns he's violently sick. For one day
he's taken all he can, physically and mentally. Mrs. Thompson
consoles him: it wasn't his fault, Alice died in an accident,
young men all get into these messes, and so on. She sees him
as the innocent victim of a designing woman, as, he realises,
everyone he knows will.

The worst part of his utter desolation is that his
brain keeps on telling him that he's very lucky, that every-

thing's worked out for the best; even for Alice's husband,
saved the expense and scandal of a divorce.
who's ~~can-now-marry-again~~ Joe will marry the princess and in-

herit the kingdom. Even if he's ~~going-to-be-miserable~~ going

to suffer all his life from a sense of guilt and frustration

and emptiness, he'll be able to suffer in comfort.

I won't consider myself too strictly bound by this

outline: the characters and the places and the material ob-

jects concerned will work out the details for themselves.

~~Income-and-environment-are-the-most-important-things~~

~~The-places~~

~~This-is-a-romantic-story.--Joe-is-the-woodcutter's~~

~~younger-son~~

The title of the story is taken from the Services

catch phrase--you it used to be chalked on tanks at the time

of the 1945 General Delection--~~of-19~~

JOE FOR KING, VOTE LABOUR! I hardly need add that this isn't

a political novel. Joe isn't very interested in politics:

being a local government officer he's ~~never-been~~ isn't allowed
join any party.
to ~~take-part-in-them.~~ He voted Labour in 1945: as he says,

the Tory candidate was related to the biggest mill-owners in

Dufton, and he was damned if he was going to lick their already

well-oiled boots.

JOE FOR KING is an exact definition of the novel's

theme. Joe is the woodcutter's younger son, who has to earn

the crown the hard way. His tragedy is that he has less tan-

gible obstacles than giants and dragons and enchanters. Less

tangible, but far harder to overcome: Alice is a dragon he

doesn't want to kill, Aunt Emily is an enchanter who wishes

nothing but his own good, and the giant is ~~the terribly intimi-~~
~~dating strength of money~~--power

~~Jack Wales' new M.G., the rigid & Hierarchy of income~~
~~the pyramid where each step upwards means the realisation of~~
~~more desires~~ the terribly intimidating power of money, with its
Cadillac, grin and voice as wheedling as Drambuie.

~~This is a noval about class the social classes the~~
~~difference between classes: so of course is any fairy story.~~

~~The novel deals with the dif~~

The novel, to put it in the baldest possible terms,
describes ~~the rise~~ a young man's rise from the working-classes.
~~Joe is nothing if not realistic; but Joe's attitude toward Joe's~~
~~methods of climbing are based upon a profound~~ Joe can't afford
to be anything else but brutally realistic in the methods he
uses to achieve his ambition. But he never loses his sense
of wonder: the story takes place, you might say, in the dark
forest round the palace.

WRITING A NOVEL

6-5-53   <u>SYNOPSIS</u>

Original Chapter 1 to be omitted.

(1)   Takes up job & home in Warley (A.M. Sept.)

(2)   Meets Cedric. Goes for walk in Warley. (P.M.)

           Sees Aston-Martin & rich man & expensive girl.

           'nothing would stop me.'

(3)   Meets Bob & Eva Sykes. Goes to Thespians. Sees

           Susan in play. ^x<u>Meets</u> Alice. (P.M. day after)

           ^xIntroduced to

(4)   BRIDGE: Getting to know Warley people (Thespian,

           Pub, (NALGO?)

(5)   Meets Eva in Library <u>then</u> Alice

           (N.B. Instead of trying to work straight through,

           I'll write, in chronological order of course, those

           chapters which are clearest in my mind. When another

           chapter seems necessary, I'll put BRIDGE as (4) &

           the information I want to convey. I'll enter this

           synopsis, or rather blueprint as I go along.)

           Alice was about 35. Fair hair, urchin cut. She was

angular, elegantly. Her breasts weren't. Sagged a little--

this more appealing than former, because real. A beautiful

voice, well-inflected, modulating actressy but not shrill.

Face always moving. Straight nose, chin tending towards heavi-

ness, sagged a little underneath. Wrinkles on her neck and

forehead. Face always moving so that sometimes she looked

monkeyish but always interesting. But a second afterwards,

John Braine

her face still as it was rarely, she'd look ugly. And then you'd look at that profile and it would make your heart break with its beauty. Good jumper, because it didn't ride up, tho' it wasn't long.

I knew she was expensive just as I'd known Susan was.
NOTE: Since I'm not going to use the going to supper at Alice's as in draft 1, Joe must meet Alice's husband on some other occasion. Little Theatre Ball? *Also introduce parents' death.

^x(Pub scene Dreffield with Charles)

^xRehearsal: Kiss

DI--Chapter 10: Lovers--OK

NB. Chapter II: Dl--OK-Rehearsal after they've become lovers.

212

WRITING A NOVEL

Decrepit debauchee, cadaverous dignity

--I should perhaps, I thought, have married Beryl.
She was more my class, my type of person. And she was so
much younger than I that in a way I'd have usurped a bourgeois
prerogative.

I've noticed that the well-to-do marry women much
younger than themselves. There have been times, in fact, when,
seeing some young girl of nineteen, still innocent, not entirely rid of adolescence's puppy fat, married to a battered &
balding bachelor of 35. I've smelt a whiff of corruption. I've
had a feeling of virginity and youth as a commodity, a tasty
dish for a jaded palate, a pawn in a game of mergers and
dividends.

After I'd finished my shopping I walked round Snow
Park, which is just behind the Market Place, ~~on the banks of~~
~~the Merton~~. The River Merton is a half-loop to the south of
Warley with Warley Forest behind it. The park is between the
river and the forest, narrowing past Market Square as if to
let the forest come nearer so that the streets end in running
water and trees. I sat down on a bench by the river and took
out the Warley Courier I'd bought. It wasn't often, I thought,
that one saw a clean river so near a town. The water was so
clear that I could see the stones on its bed. It was full
from the day's rain and running very strongly, but I could see
in a backwater about a hundred yards from where I sat, the
green scum of algae which means that water is healthy, that
fish can live in it. The seat was on a little rise sloping to

213

the river: I could see that the park ~~was-shaped-like-a-blind~~
~~letter-B-turned-towards-the-town~~ broadened out again ~~by-Squirrel~~
~~Bridge-about-a-quarter-of-a-mile-from~~ past Market Square, so
that it was in two halves, like roughly the shape of a letter
B turned away from the town.

I didn't bother about reading the paper but just sat
and looked at the river. There weren't many people about and
I could hardly hear the hum of the traffic in Market Street.
~~The-leaves-hadn't-begun-to-fall-yet;-the-forest-was-a-thick~~
~~green,-olive-evergreen-and-angelica...looking-at-it-was-as-good~~
~~as-an-eyebath.~~ Summer stayed a long time that year.

~~The-leaves-hadn't-begun-to-fall-yet;~~ the forest was
a mass of
~~thick~~ green, olive and angelica and silken where the sun caught
the wet leaves. I was on the point of lighting a cigarette but
~~didn't~~ stopped myself. There wasn't any necessity to fill in
the moment with action--it was enough to sit there, to exist.

~~After-a-while-I-left-the-seat-and-went-into-the~~
~~Market-Square.~~

I must have been sitting there for at least an hour
when the wind turned cold and I began to shiver a little.
Stalag 100
Since ~~the-POW-camp~~ I've taken no risks with colds--I've seen
too many ex-POW go down with T.B. and pneumonia--so I got up
and went into the Market Square. There was a smell of toast
and frying meat from Riley's Café, at the end of the square
nearest Snow Park. I'd been sitting too long in one position;
as I put my hand to the door I had a mild attack of pins and
needles & my leg gave under me a little, **and,** I swayed forward,
my other hand against the wall to steady myself. ~~It-was-all~~
~~over-in-a-split-second,-but-for-that-split~~

It was the most minor of minor...shock and I realised what had happened in a second; but for that second it was as if some barrier had been removed. Everything became intensely real
[xx]INSERT but for a second I felt that the ground had hit my foot. I was in a state of unreality.

but I felt rather
but the incident seemed to put everything out of focus for a second and but the incident seemed, by its jar to my conscious-ness, put everything in a different focus

Chapter before last

Goes to see Alice after rehearslas. She has car. Gives her her congé; she turns away, turns her head--Mind if I don't give you a lift?--because she doesn't want to cry in front of him.

Maybe have him tell her the truth. Not say he doesn't love her, but admit he's being bought--You too she says... you too. Well, I'm in no position to blame you. I've made a mess of everything, haven't I?

Here Tom, boyfriend of Susan, tells Joe Alice had other lovers.

Tom's father bankrupt. Joe, on walk one evening after studying.

He was very drunk. 'I don't like you, Thompson. You've heard the news I suppose?'

'You won't starve,' I said. I didn't feel in the least sorry for him. He'd have more money in the bank now than I had. 'You're glad, aren't you?' he said. 'I don't give a damn whether you live or die,' I said.

'I ought to smash your face in,' he growled. I felt
an answering violence rising inside me but repressed it. 'Listen, Smith I've moved in rougher circles than you. You wouldn't
have it all your own way. Of course, the publicity would be a
great help to your father--'

'You're clever, aren't you? he sneered. 'Clever
enough to get round old Brown too...'

Last Chapter

I thought that only one person could understand what
happened between Mrs. T. and I, & that was Alice.

I'd to strain to catch the words. 'You made her
happy. But I know you killed her.' '<u>What's that</u>?' 'You
killed her.' 'Don't be a bloody fool. I wasn't with her. I
never would have wished her any harm.' 'You killed her. Directly or indirectly, it doesn't matter.'

'You don't know,' I said. 'It's no good digging up
the dead. I won't say anything about it at the inquest if
that's what you're afraid of. I don't see that you need come
into it.' That was big of him: if any scandal were unearthed
he'd have his fair share. But it was no use annoying him: he
was in a queer mood.

--As if Warley going mad?--

(1)   Warley--lodgings. Meets...<u>Beryl</u>

(2)   Little Theatre--<u>Meet</u> Alice, Susan in play

(3)   Meets Alice TH--in play...

(4)   Rehearsals--talks with Susan

	(5)	Rehearsals--kisses Alice
	(6)	Become lovers
	~~(7)-------Party~~	
	~~(8)-------Quarrels-Takes-out-Susan~~	
7	~~(9)-------Quarrels-with-Alice.~~	Rehearsals...
8	~~(6)-(7)---Party~~ PARTY	
9	(8)	Charles Dreffield
10	~~(9)-------Quarrels-with-Alice.~~	Takes out Susan.
11	(10)	Quarrels with Alice
12	(11)	Scene with Tardoff. ('I had in fact taken her out several times.')
13	(12)	Civic Ball--goes off with Beryl.
14	(14)	Makes it up with Alice
	(15)	Weekend, in London with A.
	(16)	Letter from Susan who's gone away. Realises still OK with her.
	(17)	Out with Susan
	(18)	A change in Tardoff's attitude--nasty, tough. 'To hell with him. I'd
	(19)	Go away. And besides Alice was talking marriage.
	(20)	Brown calls into office, Joe attends to him. 'I'm going away.'
	(21)	Brown says don't go, etc.
	(22)	Scene with Susan's boyfriend
	(23)	Scene with Alice.
	(24)	Last Chapter

The novel was finished, under the title of *Joe for King*, in September 1955, just before I was married. We lived in furnished rooms in Newbiggin-by-the-Sea, a small fishing port on the North-East coast. There's a coal mine there, but it's closed down now. I was the librarian for the new county branch, which was about half a mile from our home along the promenade. There was always a cold wind from the North Sea, even in summer. It was an inbred, clannish community, mostly miners and fishermen. I felt completely isolated, my career, such as it was, as a librarian at an end, my future as a writer in the balance.

I still daydreamed of success, of being a professional novelist, of being a *Name*; it was all that kept me going. And in the spring the letter from my agent arrived to tell me that *Joe for King* had been accepted as it stood; the only alteration asked for was the title. Although it was to be over a year before I gave up librarianship for full-time writing, my real life, the one I was born for, began that day.

I didn't make any fuss about changing the title. Its origin was the fact that the district in which Joe has a room is called the Top. The other associations of the phrase immediately came to mind. It was Daniel Webster who coined it, referring to the shortage of talent in the legal profession. Joe for King, a wartime catchphrase (it's referred to in the novel), wouldn't have done at all. I often wonder now whether the book would have been so successful if the publisher, Maurice Temple-Smith, hadn't seen just how impossible it was. And if he hadn't recognised how exactly right *Room at the Top* was. I didn't do it all by myself.

And that's a thought to leave you with. The reader employed by my literary agent didn't consider the novel publishable. My literary agent had faith in me; he went ahead, even after four leading publishers had turned it down. And then, even after Maurice Temple-Smith had accepted it, other members of the firm didn't think that it was their sort of novel. Since he was new to the firm, they decided it was only fair to give him his chance. It turned out very well for him; but if it hadn't, it would have been a black mark against him right at the start.

None of this is within your control. Having thought about it, forget it. Only the work itself is within your control. Put the work first, and the right people will emerge to help you. Whenever you're depressed about the work remember that once it's finished help is waiting. Treasure it when you receive it.

NOTES

[1] John Braine, *The Queen of a Distant Country* (Eyre Methuen, 1972), p. 94.

[2] Norman Podhoretz, *Making It* (Jonathan Capé, 1968), pp. 139–41.

[3] *The Writers' and Artists' Year Book* (Adam & Charles Black, annually).

[4] John O'Hara, *The Ewings* (Hodder and Stoughton, 1972), pp. 184–85.

[5] F. Scott Fitzgerald, *The Great Gatsby*, in *The Bodley Head Scott Fitzgerald*, Volume One (The Bodley Head, 1958), pp. 197–98.

[6] Anthony Powell, *The Acceptance World* (Penguin, 1962), pp. 11–12.

[7] Graham Greene, *A Burnt-Out Case* (Penguin, 1963), p. 9.

[8] *Ibid.*, p. 11.

[9] *Ibid.*, pp. 11–12.

[10] Anthony Powell, *A Question of Upbringing* (Penguin, 1962), pp. 7–8.

[11] *Ibid.*, p. 9.

[12] John O'Hara, *Appointment in Samarra* (Pan, 1958), pp. 5–6.

[13] *Ibid.*, pp. 7–9.

[14] *Ibid.*, p. 14.

[15] Alan Sillitoe, *Saturday Night and Sunday Morning* (Pan, 1960), p. 5.

[16] *Ibid.*, p. 7.

[17] James Joyce, *Ulysses* (The Bodley Head, 1960), pp. 13–16.

[18]Nancy Mitford, *Noblesse Oblige* (Hamish Hamilton, 1956).

[19]Anthony Powell, *A Buyer's Market* (Penguin, 1962), pp. 34–35.

[20]John Braine, *Room at the Top* (Eyre & Spottiswoode, 1957), pp. 176–77.

[21]Anthony Powell, *At Lady Molly's* (Penguin, 1963), p. 59.

[22]*Ibid.*, p. 60.

[23]F. Scott Fitzgerald, *The Crack-Up*, in *The Bodley Head Scott Fitzgerald*, Volume One (The Bodley Head, 1958), p. 278.

[24]Stuart Chase, *The Tyranny of Words* (Harcourt, Brace & World, Inc., 1938).

[25]*Ibid.*, p. 9.

[26]*Ibid.*, p. 10.

[27]John Braine, *op. cit.*, pp. 250–51.

[28]*Ibid.*, p. 79.

[29]F. Scott Fitzgerald, *The Great Gatsby*, p. 155.

[30]John Braine, *op. cit.*, pp. 91–92.

[31]Donald Hamilton, *Death of a Citizen* (Coronet, 1966), pp. 34–35.

[32]Irving Wallace, *The Writing of One Novel* (New English Library/Mentor, 1972), p. 29.

[33]*Ibid.*

[34]John O'Hara, *From the Terrace* (Random House, 1958), pp. 472–73.

[35]Anthony Powell, *The Acceptance World*, pp. 65–67.

[36]*Ibid.*, p. 68.

[37]*Ibid.*, p. 87.

[38]*Ibid.*, p. 103.

[39]*Ibid.*, pp. 132–33.

[40]*Ibid.*, p. 133.

[41]John Braine, *The Crying Game* (Eyre & Spottiswoode, 1968), pp. 143–44.

[42]F. Scott Fitzgerald, *The Great Gatsby*, p. 234.

[43] *Ibid.*, pp. 253–54.

[44] D. H. Lawrence, *A Selection from Phoenix*, A. A. H. Inglis, ed. (Penguin/Peregrine, 1971), pp. 163–66.